Cannot Stay:
Essays on Travel

Also by Kevin Oderman

White Vespa

Going

How Things Fit Together

Ezra Pound and the Erotic Medium

Cannot Stay

Essays on Travel

Kevin Oderman

etruscan press

Etruscan Press

Wilkes University

84 West South Street

Wilkes-Barre, PA 18766

(570) 408-4546

www.etruscanpress.org

Published 2015 by Etruscan Press
Printed in the United States of America
Cover design, interior design, and typesetting by L. Elizabeth Powers
The text of this book is set in Adobe Garamond
First Edition

15 16 17 18 19 5 4 3 2 1

Library of Congress Cataloguing-in-Publication Data

Oderman, Kevin, 1950- author.
[Essays. Selections]
Cannot stay : essays on travel / Kevin Oderman. -- First edition.
pages cm
SBN 978-0-9897532-8-9
1. Oderman, Kevin, 1950---Travel. 2. Voyages and travels. I. Oderman, Kevin, 1950-
White amber. Container of (work): II. Title.
G465.O3225 2015
910.4--dc23

2014037085

Please turn to the back of this book for a list of the sustaining funders of Etruscan Press.

for Ambrose Oderman, father and traveler

We all walk the long road, cannot stay.
— Eddie Vedder, "The Long Road"

Cannot Stay

Acknowledgments

The author gratefully acknowledges the journals where these essays first appeared: "White Amber," "Judith and Harold," "Puppet Heads," "Waiting for the Bombs," and "At Koré's" in the *Northwest Review*; "Time to Kill: Cambodia" and "A House Fitting" in the *Southwest Review*; "Selling" in the *North Dakota Quarterly*; "Colors" in *Green Mountains Review*; "Of Corse" in the *Tusculum Review;* and "Trips Not Taken" in *Shadowbox*.

I am indebted to the Fulbright Scholar Program and to West Virginia University for time and a warrant to travel; to Phil Brady, Jackie Fowler, Bill Schneider, and the entire inspired tribe at Etruscan, who made this book possible.

A profound bow to my old mentors who, in classrooms or in letters, awakened me: Judah Bierman, Georgia Crampton, Donald Pearce, Sherman Paul, and Guy Davenport.

I have been supported in all this, the traveling and the writing, by friends. You cannot know how much your friendship has mattered. Finally, how lucky I am to have found her, my touchstone at home and occasional companion on the road, Sara Pritchard, aka Delta B. Horne.

Kevin Oderman

Cannot Stay:
Essays on Travel

INTRODUCTION

::

Check in. A subdued line of passengers, everybody waiting their turn. Someone pushes a small bag forward, eyeing with a smirk the woman with the luggage trolley. It's always so. And yet, even that woman is traveling light, leaving behind far more than she could ever pack into a few suitcases. By necessity, the traveler gives up on things, preferring for a time the experience of going. And part of the attraction of travel, it turns out, is getting free of all that stuff, which, however desirable in prospect, encumbers you. Having left almost everything behind, you walk lighter in the new place, nothing to tend to but the few things in your luggage.

Thinking about travel, it's easy to skip over the actual getting there. The hasty curbside goodbye under the sign for departures. The bout of heartache. Few people enjoy the airports and the long flights, over seas. Over there, you think, the real traveling will begin, but even pushing through the heavy doors at the airport, you've already begun to be someone else. You hardly notice, perhaps, the subtle change, the traveler emerging from behind your at-home self. Traveling by air, you suffer a series of familiar rituals. You're searched, you wait, you pass through one straight gate after another. You're bound to your seat. The flight attendants repeat the grave incantations. You're asked to consider the dire *what ifs*. Then you're flying, actually flying, and you succumb to the Mesmer thrum of the jets. Libations are poured. In a spell, perhaps, you try to imagine your passage as seen from the ground—something silver, needling its way through the sky. The trance deepens.

If air travel seems no more than a parody of ceremony, it works. It not only takes you to a different place, in the obvious sense, but traveling, you undergo a metamorphosis. The person you are at home no longer feels entirely convincing. Perhaps because you're a bit disoriented, your at-home self suddenly seems at least half a habit, mostly made in response to circumstances you've now left behind—your everyday life. Stepping outside the terminal, you feel it might be possible to just walk away from all that. Some feel this, I fear, as an invitation to bad behavior, to run amok out of hearing. Some do. But you might feel the real chances are inward, that in travel you have the opportunity to recall a younger you, a self less hemmed in by social identities. And you find in traveling that the world comes to you less filtered. Your senses seem sharper— like that happy moment when you try on the new glasses with the new prescription, and you find you can see again the way you did when you were young. You walk out of the terminal, the world buzzing around you, and you strike out into it, just a traveler.

About twenty years ago I was given the chance to live for a season in Thessaloniki, in Greece, and I took it, going alone. I turned off the path of the life I'd been living. I traveled a great deal from Thessaloniki, on the Greek mainland, out to the islands, the Sporades, the Cyclades, the Dodecanese, up to Bulgaria, and twice into Turkey. I didn't realize, as it was happening, that I was becoming a traveler, but I've been traveling ever since. Not all the time, but often. Around the Mediterranean, the Balkans and the Baltics, Southeast Asia, Pakistan, Nepal and Sri Lanka,

Bali, Japan. Many places. But I hope I haven't become worldly. I want to be always impressionable, and one of the things I love best about travel is that I'm more impressionable abroad than at home.

This is a book of journeys. Most books about travel describe the great arc of one heroic adventure or the rewards and frustrations of digging deep in one place. Travel literature is rich with wonderful books of both sorts. While this is the kind of travel we most often read about, it's not the kind of travel we often do. I travel when I can, trips of two or three weeks, a month maybe. The essays in this book have grown out of such trips, have been called up by the various worlds I've been lucky enough to travel through. But as much as to places, these essays speak to the experience of travel, to what it means to shake loose of your at-home identity, to carry all you need of your life in a worn daypack, to step footloose into a world unfamiliar, and in doing so, to catch a glimpse of where you've come from as a strange place, too.

WHITE AMBER

::

The sudden spring. Twilight at 11:00 p.m. and twilight at 2:00 a.m. A spring condensed in the far north, the bloom on, the different new greens, from near yellow through chartreuse to leaf green to pine. The beautiful woods, the silver birches in the road cut, behind them the red-barked small pines and a tree I don't know, its trunk the color of old pewter and its new leaves ruddy, that other green, the blood of spring. This is the third week of May, this is the Baltic coast, the cold sea, gray or steel blue, just there. This bus driving through the rushing season. Two weeks ago the ground was rough with ice, they say. Now the birdhouses are loud with cheeping. Arriving in the bloom and not long for this place, it will always be spring here for me.

Forest and farmsteads. Around the farm buildings the brightest thing the stacks of new-cut firewood, silver and salmon, opened by the raw strokes of the axe. It won't always be spring for the farmers, already wood-making for next winter, winter just past. The fields green, green, or a new-tilled brown, or absolute yellow, rape seed in flower, I think, not sure, not knowing much for sure, passing through.

This is the day earth promised in darkness. Now, the earth speaks glory. The little leaves like girls, boys, so small and frail, alive with the first impulse. I look through glass at all that, going by, my own face white with winter, reflected, still, in front of the rushing, renewed world. This is age, and to age earth speaks a different word.

::

Vilnius

Everything bent—in the old town, anyway, and this is what I've come for, to be reminded that the built world hasn't always been so square. Streets plotted on a grid, structures obeying the rule, I get tired of it. I begin to desire that other thing, buildings bending with the arc of an alley, most every building connected with the building next door. And I find myself packing a bag, setting out, just to walk such streets. They must have seemed like good streets to walk for a long time, for millennia. If you take the long view, my desire can hardly be construed as eccentric. Yet we rarely do take the long view, and I too was surprised when years ago I visited ancient Akrotiri on Santorini. The old town there is very old, Minoan, buried in ash like Pompeii but some seventeen hundred years before catastrophe rained from the sky at the foot of Vesuvius. Ancient Akrotiri is an archaeological site now, and the eruption that buried it left ash so deep that you enter the town by walking down, into the ground. The archaeologists have had the site roofed, which is estranging, but in spite of that what startles at ancient Akrotiri is just how familiar, how old-towny, the place seems. I remember how arrested I felt, walking into the little triangular "square," where the alleys meet in an irregular junction, registering the absolute rightness of that place, knowing it had been a place of chance meetings, of assignations, of talk, thirty-six hundred years ago. But ancient Akrotiri, while uniquely well preserved, was not the first such town. It would have been already the inheritor of a mature building tradition, originating who knows where or when but imagined out of the ground by people finding a way to live together.

In Vilnius, the imagining was not done all at once, either. But, I'd been hearing for years that the old towns of the Baltic capitals were largely intact, as if stilled in amber through the long centuries, and I'd come to have a look, to see if the towns would answer, would speak to my desire to find myself again walking the curved alleys of what feels like memory. My expectations were tempered, however; I knew no place is exempt from time, from history, and certainly not the capitals of Lithuania, or Latvia, or Estonia, where armies have marched, to and fro, for centuries.

In Vilnius, I've found a room off Bernardinu, in a quiet and irregular courtyard, where an old woman shuffles out in her slippers to arrange her laundry on a few yards of clothesline several times a day. I don't forget her when I walk through the passageway out to Bernardinu, into streets dominated by people decidedly young. The old town in Vilnius is being restored. It has been undergoing a major restoration for years, another kind of springtime, I guess, but restoration displaces old people even as it renews the old buildings. The old town in Vilnius has only been partially restored, but the old people have long since retreated into ramshackle courtyards. They walk the expensive streets looking dispossessed, looking more out of place than the tourists.

On Bernardinu, I walk down. At first the sweep is right and then a long leftward curve, down to Pilies Gatve—Castle Street—the main artery of old Vilnius. Crossing under the arch over Benardinu onto Pilies, I step out of the quiet of a residential street into the commotion of a world public and commercial. Pilies has always had a commercial character, and here *always* is a long time. Many of the buildings still standing on the cobbled street date from the sixteenth century. But maybe not the cobbles themselves, which look too cleanly cut for old. The shape of the street itself, however, has the real old-feel, the way it tapers and widens, like something grown. I walk up it often, admiring the buildings. Pedestrians dominate the street, a few walking fast, going somewhere, but many more strolling. Their own paths up or down the sinuous street shift side to side as whim suggests. I wonder if Pilies Gatve has ever before in its long history looked so gay, so bright. Closely tended, the stucco facades of the buildings all are smooth, and the paint as delicious looking as the tubs in an ice cream shop, yellow and mint green, raspberry and sherbet orange, a blueberry purple, a vanilla white, and one blackish building, suggesting licorice.

Whether the buildings are Gothic or Baroque, they each have a share in the pastel paint that contributes so strongly to the feel of the street. The colors scroll by as you walk, striped by shadows and lit by the watery light of the far north angling in over the rooftops. Pilies must be the most fully renovated street in the old town, and it raises the question, of course, about what's really old here, not the plaster, not the paint, not the paving stones; the surfaces are new, as are many of the businesses: trendy restaurants and shops, some shops dealing exclusively in amber. And yet, the old still informs these places, deeper than skin. The surfaces must have been renewed many times, after all, in five hundred years. But the shape of things, the deeper patterns, have persisted, and now are the very reason that the surfaces are renewed, for tourists who flock to see the place, for natives who feel that the identity of their city is bound up in the old irregularities of these streets. Still, the feeling that the newness of the surfaces impairs the authenticity of the old town is no doubt widespread. Here and there, I see places where the restorers have left neat cutouts in the new stucco to reveal the *real* old bricks or stones underneath, which tacitly acknowledges the difficulties.

Still, I like walking in color, the gold trapezoids of reflected light shimmering on the streets, on the walls. And later, standing in weather suddenly threatening, I can hardly credit how gorgeous the Baroque spires of St. Catherine's look, picked out by the sun, pink and white against a blue-black sky. Then the rain does fall. Still, I feel lucky to have seen the big pink church in such a light. But the odds are good for such luck in Vilnius; the low skyline is thick with spires, towers, belfries, and domes. Strolling the ever-turning lanes of the old town, they loom up suddenly, and often, and drop from sight just as suddenly. An old-town layout makes small provision for broad vistas. Perhaps this is one of the attractions, the way the turning streets serve up a new prospect every few steps, and in Vilnius this impression is strengthened by the changing paint, the ribbon of ice cream colors unscrolling on either side of the street.

Back in my room, I look out into the half-light of what feels like it should be night but is not. The laundry is in. I've been out walking all day long. Several days. On the bent streets I now know my way, if not at every turn, at most. The maze is coming down. The heightened attention that a maze calls up, that itself brightens or darkens the world, would ease, and I would be a familiar of this place, if I were staying on. But I'm a traveler, and soon I'll be exploring different streets, in Tallinn. I'll be leaving with a little of the strangeness still on.

Strangeness is good, almost our only hope against the opacity of presumption, that thick lens. I've been wondering about why I'm here. I've been wondering about what this kind of travel is all about. I know my desire to walk the bent streets is a shared desire, that the place itself has been restored to call out to the likes of me, to tourists. Perhaps that's troubling, in a way, the familiar irony: that the authenticity of the Baltic old towns is threatened by the people who come to see them, and by the people catering to those visitors, until the whole place becomes so ersatz you might as well be touring Las Vegas. But that's just so, and the dynamics not so hard to understand. The desire that's catered to, however, is harder to touch. I suppose that whipping boy Romanticism will have to take another turn at the post, that the hard but true realities of the industrial and now the postindustrial age will be seen to have called up yet again sentimental reconstructions of what was and has been lost. And likely there is something to that, but this argument is so dismissive it discourages thinking; indeed, it discourages making the trip. Still, we take these journeys. And for the most part the impulse to visit goes unexamined, travel in and of itself is seen as a sufficient reason to go, and this is perhaps the most obscuring presumption of all.

Okay, I admit to having a theory about the attraction. It takes for granted that life at home doesn't entirely satisfy, that if it did we wouldn't take to the roads. Of course, life lets us down in any number of ways, personal ways, but I'm thinking now about something bigger than that, something cultural, which is not to single out our ways as peculiarly deficient. The deficiency, according to my theory, must be universal. As far back as I can remember, it has seemed self-evident to me that people are fundamentally the same now as they ever were, that a baby transported across the millennia into this now would grow up just as modern as the rest of us. And, to turn it around, send a baby back five or ten thousand years, perhaps even thirty thousand years, and that baby would find its way into the culture there, would grow to be an adult of that time. Rather than a Paiute trailing a travois through the alkaline dust of the Great Basin, a man signing for a box on his front porch, making small talk with the guy from UPS. Rather than a man twisting the top off a bottle of seltzer, a man carrying a water jug through a low door in Harappa, in the Indus valley, five thousand years ago. Sitting down with a cheap paperback in front of the gas logs, or a monk isolating himself in the rock hills over the Egyptian desert. Driving I-68 over the mountains and on toward D.C., or navigating the Australian outback by the songlines. Writing, or way back, spraying pigment through a straw at my splayed hand to leave a print on a wall in a cave in what we now call France. The accident of our birth, we say, meaning the when and the where and the to whom. And perhaps I don't mean much more than that, just to acknowledge that whatever, whoever we are when our head crowns into this world, who and what we become is wildly dependent on that when and where. Soon enough the culture and the life-ways so fuse with that baby born into the world under prairie stars, or in a mud house in a Moroccan oasis, or in an American hospital, that all those other ways of being human, the great panoply of possible lives that newborn could have lived, get lost. I was a baby brought home to a white ranch house in a blue blanket in 1950, in Portland, Oregon; that was my accident. Out of the ways of being human, this way.

In saying *yes* to one way of living we say *no* to the myriad. *No* to a life of herding or hunting, *no* to seafaring, *no* to the raven people set flying by their shaman. *No* to the outcast, to the Untouchable, to life before the wheel. People we could have been, were, in fact, *ready to be* when we entered this world.

Was that sea of potential exhausted in making the one fish? Is the oblivion absolute? Or do we walk in a crowd of ghosts, our unrealized lives, their whispering a murmur just out of hearing? Not ghosts, maybe, but I think there is sometimes a responsiveness that has more to do with our unrealized potentials than with who we've become. Mostly the voices are the quiet voices of muted yearning, but occasionally they clamor, and one voice rises up to shout, *Yes, yes; I didn't realize such worlds existed when I said no to this.*

We hear these voices most when traveling, away from the circumstances that half make us who we are; and, traveling alone, we hear them louder, no one there to remind us of our confining self. So travel attracts us, attracts me, by appealing to potentials that have gone unexpressed. Of course, we travel through space, time no more than the duration of the trip. It's *right now* everywhere, sure. Time travel remains impossible. But that *now* is not simple; the life-ways of times long gone in one place are still practiced in another. In that sense, time is uneven. You don't have to travel long to find fields worked with white bullocks, to watch the seeds of the coming harvest broadcast from human hands, to see offerings of rice and fruit, wicks burning in butter, rather than a tray going round fluttering with rumpled dollars. This is a reason for travel.

And life as it was lived leaves a mark, sometimes a distinct mark, in old buildings, old neighborhoods built to answer the needs of those other ways, a tradition and aesthetic ours no more. Walking such streets doesn't always have to do with the past, but, responding, we sense something unused in us now, almost lost in the life we are living. This is good to know, even if, returning home, we seem to be restored to our former selves.

In Vilnius, the impulse to restore has called up, it seems almost at once, the impulse to vandalize. If Pilies Gatve keeps its paint refreshed, most of the old town alleys have been defaced by graffiti. It's easy to imagine the sound of spray cans being shaken while the painters with rollers and brushes are still in sight, carrying their ladders away.

::

Tallinn

I arrive in Tallinn under the weather, with a headache. Migrainous, if not migraine. My inner weather mixes with the skies of Tallinn like soap and water shaken in a jar, gas fumes rising off a puddle, heat waves off a tarred road. A cloud rippling like a flag in the mind. Sick, too sick to see straight. In a less nauseous moment, I somehow manage to get to my room on Uus. By midnight, though I still hurt, the world has separated from me and looks stable out there, if ghostly, in the peculiar pallor of Tallinn's white nights. It is the weekend, the few revelers who pass by sound loud enough for giants, big voiced and rudely made.

In the morning, the drinkers have given way to small herds of folk trailing behind tour guides, each with a number held aloft on a stick. I think of birds in flocks, the way they turn, of the bellwether, ant highways, ways of moving together. I let them walk on by and then pick my way through two-hearted Tallinn like an invalid. Tallinn has two old towns—Toompea, the administrative town, on the high ground, and, below and toward the harbor, the much larger mercantile town. On a map, the towns look like a cell about to divide. Walking, the difference is altitude. Toompea looks out over its city walls, the lower town does not. And after a quick circuit of Toompea, I head back down, preferring the alley called the "short leg" not only for its name (the alternative route is the "long leg," after all), but because it's steep and crooked. In spite of the reputed attractiveness of big views, it's the lower town in Tallinn that gets the crowds.

From outside, it's hard to get a comprehensive look at the Holy Spirit Church. Air transport would be required. From street level, if the structure stands out, it's only because it's painted a severe white. Tourists with cameras generally settle for a photo of the clock face that overlooks the small and triangular Great Guild Square, or they stand and shoot up, taking a picture of the corby-step gable and the spire. In spite of that spire, the white church has a squat look, as if it had hunched down among its neighbors and held on, for almost seven hundred years. But inside, the massive limestone walls and pillars are rendered almost weightless. I'm not sure how. The groined ceiling vaults have the feel of nine tents pitched in the open, in a field maybe, so distant do the adjoining buildings seem. In Tallinn, I visited the Holy Spirit Church many times. I studied it, I submitted to it. I watched the light shift with time and weather. I listened to a concert, a boy's choir, the timbre of the little boys' voices the very quiver of innocent flesh. I made friends with the cat that sometimes prowled there, scratching its belly as it sat next to me in a pew. I stood at the back, listening to a sermon.

I want to praise the Church of the Holy Spirit, but the terms elude me. Perhaps it's not so hard to describe. The plank floors, all the finish gone except tight against the pews, where it shows dark brown. The simple, blackened oak of the pews themselves. The still light. I want to use the word *sober* as a term of praise. And *serious*. And *quiet*. A place for the small, honest voices to be heard, of conscience, of simple recognition, and of welcome. Nothing for show, no reaching, not even for heaven. There is room here for sorrow, that good sadness we can't resist and really live.

In the tradition of almshouse churches, the Church of the Holy Spirit has a main and a side aisle. The main aisle is centered on the choir, in which stands the fifteenth century altar, the work of Bernt Notke and his workshop in Lubeck. The altar is a triptych with double, folding wings. Fully open, the way I see it, the altar reveals carved and polychrome figures. The central panel depicts the Pentecost, the apostles clustered around Mary, who looks up to receive the gift of the Holy Spirit. The mood expectant, the scene hushed. The altar, the only thing in the church that could be called splendid, stands back in the choir, at a considerable remove from the main hall. Close, it might be too much. But although Mary looks beautiful against her gold robe and the gilt plaque of her halo, there is something of the puppet in the apostles, something naïve. And this naïve quality sits well with the church hall, where the primary decorations are the simple, painted illustrations of biblical stories.

When I walk down the aisles, the church goes in motion, the pillars on either side move in front of the walls, in front of the barrel vaults in the walls. The pillars support the shallow raised choirs that run the length of the church and connect visually with the organ loft at the back. A great rail runs in front of the choirs and the loft, on three sides, and it is this rail that is divided into the painted panels, the biblical illustrations—Noah preparing for the flood, the rainbow sign, an Annunciation, Christ baptized, Christ walking on water under a brown sky—over sixty in all. The illustrations on the rail and the railing itself are painted in a restricted palette, somewhat like the Baltic woods would look in full summer. Ivy green and olive; burnt sienna; brown; a little muted red; a dark, watery blue, dense enough to float an ark, for a man to stroll on. Supported by the brown pillars, the whole suggests a forest canopy, as if in the hall you stood in a meadow, under peaked pavilions, and looked out at surrounding trees. This would be the church for me, if only.

I stand for a moment in the doorway, in the thin light of evening. Then I am walking, and walking I remember a line of poetry, written about the time the church was built, by Charles d'Orleans, a prisoner then, in England. "My ghostly fader, I me confesse." That word, *ghostly*, for holy, that is what calls up the old poet. A presence felt but not seen, or if seen, just glimpsed. Something apparitional, just fading from sight. A white reflection before the glass goes clear. The ground under your feet, sinking away. Or to wake in the night reaching out for a disappearing world. So much of what we sense, what we want, won't hold still for our embrace. And we are left to live in the tangible world, a world that at least persists in seeming to be there.

Here, too, the ice cream colors, even sorbets, orange and raspberry sorbet, the colors too intense to admit an admixture of cream. The alleys bending, curvaceous, the old buildings again made smooth. Everything beautiful in the long evening. Another day I visit the church of St. Nicholas, now a museum. Not all the old churches have been reconsecrated after the half-century of communism. I take my time. Here, too, there are altarpieces with double wings—or as they are also called, shutters. And I notice how one, from the workshop of Adriane Issenbraut, painted around 1515, features a crucifixion in the foreground, and a panorama of Jerusalem behind, blued by distance, a walled Jerusalem that looks suspiciously like Tallinn. I don't hurry, I walk on, and after a while I find myself in a crowd of school children, just as I am sitting down in front of another work by Bernt Notke, his justly praised *Dance of Death*. The children's teacher stands in front of us, lecturing, pointing first at the lively dead dressed in their winding sheets, then at one or another of the living, the Cardinal, the Emperor, the Empress, the Pope, or the King. I am amused that in the painting it is the living who look the stiffs, while the dead rock on. The children, in their matching uniforms, try to attend, to follow what their teacher is saying, but wide-eyed, the hum of their own lives is just too much for them; they can't listen for long. Then the teacher calls the kids to order and marches them away, leaving me alone with the high-stepping, dancing dead. I consider them. The world the living in the painting knew has gone with them. And Bernt Notke's warning looks to go unheeded at St. Nicholas. The museumgoers walk the length of the twenty-five-foot panel, not afraid. Not one of them seems to heed the warning, looks as nervous as the Cardinal or the King, nor raises a hand overhead to dance a step or two with the dead, who are perhaps too dead, too long dead, to have the force of poor Yorick for Hamlet, who "knew him." I think I see the tourists in the picture, though, in the background, in the two oblivious strollers out walking their scampering dogs. Still, our eyes often bear false witness. It's more than likely that at least some of the old, and perhaps even some of the young, walk in front of that *Dance* with a dead friend.

::

Riga

Here, the trolleys are still running. The time of trolleys is still now, and I ride them daily, thinking it was a good time and a time not so distant that I can't remember trolleys in Portland, where I grew up, raining sparks down from the wires strung overhead. They've brought *light rail* back to Portland, in a very limited way, but in Riga the trolleys never left. Screech and clangor, forty cents for any ride, which is good, as my ride out to Mezaparks, where I'm staying, takes me clear to the end of the line.

In Riga, too, the old town is the big attraction, the alleys and squares set with tables and chairs for the trade. But there are not so many old buildings here, and I know why. I've seen the photos, the old town bombed out and looking a sad ruin by the end of WWII. What remains is the plat of the streets, a few old buildings, and a lot of infill, some of it attractive, without a doubt. But perhaps even the plat is not as interesting as in the other Baltic capitals. It is less sinuous, less bent, and the whole of the old town smaller and enclosed by something a lot like a rectangle. What's left has been made to accommodate itself to a modern grid. Which is not to say Riga isn't an attractive city, it is; there is a great deal more to Riga than the old town, and the old town is pleasant enough. I enjoy walking there.

Still, the signature building in old Riga is the House of the Blackheads, a guild building originally constructed in the fourteenth century, but rebuilt from the ground up very recently, the job called done in 1999. The House of the Blackheads stands on Town Square, and it looks both old and new. It must be camera friendly, as it is by far the most photographed building I have seen in the Baltic States. Someone, it seems, is always taking its picture, and at times the square is circumscribed by a great arc of tourists turning their cameras on its fantastic façade. Or façades, as it has two, an artifact of an addition to the original Gothic structure in the nineteenth century that more or less mimicked the medieval building. Each has elaborate stepped gables in stone and matching stone window and door surrounds, which show brightly against the red brick of the buildings proper. But honestly, the brick is too new to be called red; it's still bright orange. And bells and whistles! The blue and gilt clock face, the small forest of decorative crosses and spires climbing up the gables, the statues. It's not modern, but part of what the House of the Blackheads is is new. Rebuilt for the eight-hundredth anniversary of the founding of the city, the building clearly makes a claim for history, or against history, depending on how you want to look at it.

I step down off the trolley on Brivibis and walk toward Gertrudes Street, ready to have a look at some of the most renowned of Riga's Art Nouveau buildings. And the buildings are there, on Elizabetes Street and Alberta, far and wide, really, great blocks of buildings not shy about decoration. Most of these buildings are large apartments, built to accommodate Riga's burgeoning population in the late nineteenth and early twentieth centuries. The timing proved fortunate. The buildings are attractive still, decked out in a wild array of motifs, classical, Gothic, Egyptian, and more. Artful low-relief work and freestanding statues, glazed tiles, and, especially, beautiful doors. The streets are wide, the buildings low. The population is dense enough to support sidewalks busy with pedestrians, the best thing about a modern city, I often think. Somehow, on busy sidewalks the energy of the crowd becomes your energy, and you feel as if you can keep going longer, farther. And I don't think that feeling is an illusion.

But the energy is frenetic, and finally, I have to admit, I'd rather go less far but quietly, and less in the company of cars. On Alberta Iela, I get my wish, the street silent, almost deserted. I linger with the pair of sphinxes guarding the entry to the apartment at #2, watching leaf shadows play over their black faces. I look first to my left, and then right, the street straight end to end, and I miss already the bent streets of the old towns. I've lived my life on straight streets; whatever they have to say—about geometry or the strict line perhaps—I've heard enough of it. I like the decorative facades of Art Nouveau; they make me look around, forget for a while the linear prospects. The beautiful details, the great, vertical slashes of red tiles in the façade at #2. "God is in the details," as Mies van der Rohe, famously, if oddly, remarked, since the buildings he and his fellow moderns designed came so perilously close to not having any.

So I gravitate back to Riga's old town, where, after all, a fair amount of the infill is Art Nouveau. I don't fail to notice the low-relief peacock on

Smilsu or, just down the street, over a door, the gorgeous, sleepy face of a woman, her eyes closed, her ears hidden each under an elaborately carved curl, her mouth pursed as if she were tasting a melancholy truth. Weary, I long for her beauty, to rest in it. I decide to sit down for coffee, in a small square; I take a table inside, hoping for a break from all the bustle. Nodding in front of my espresso, I drift toward reverie, one of the attractions of traveling alone, a luxury, to court the imagination, to indulge a reverie that is sometimes abetted by weariness. But not this time. The door swings wide and in they strut, the louts. I've heard of their kind, bands of *bucks* who fly to the Baltics just to drink and make rowdy. English, this crowd, and they hardly look real. Somehow, they've been inflated into something outsize. Steroids, maybe. But big, all of them, and for sure rowdy. They've come in for the bathroom and crowd into the tiny cubicle several at a time, brushing off the protests of the wait staff. Then they swagger out, still buckling up, a couple exposing themselves for fun or maybe just failing to notice. They bully everyone. They talk loud, loud as shouting, but it is just talk. They sit down at tables with people they don't know, tickle the chins of little girls and babies. No one dares confront them, the louts in the orange T-shirts. They have a leader, smaller, smarter. They do what he says, their Mephisto. Dressed in white overalls and pink gym shoes, he wears a green wig and has powdered his face, painted his eyebrows white. His jibes are witty and malicious, way more witty than what the locals are going to be able to appreciate in English. He is the only one of them who doesn't project a wild, pulsing energy. He seems at ease in a relaxed malevolence. Is it the orange shirts that make me think of *Clockwork Orange*, or just their sociopathic glee? They dare you to admit you want them to leave. They draw out their exit beyond what is bearable until, like every bully you have ever known, they stomp out and are gone.

If, in walking the streets of the old town, I sometimes feel the ghostly presence of a me who might have lived in such a place, long ago, I have to acknowledge that the opposite is also true, that the people who walked here then, when the old streets were new, already carried in them the unfulfilled potential to live a life much like mine. And I too must carry in me potential ways of living that some future, had I been born into it, would have called into being. And perhaps this future self is the ghostliest self of all, the most unknowable. Still, imagining futures has its attractions, as it must have for Anthony Burgess and Stanley Kubrick, when they conjured up the *Clockwork Orange*, and occasionally the supposers do turn out to have gotten it right. But I don't think about the future very much, a time in which I, of necessity, will have no better part than one of Bert Notke's dancing dead. And somehow I need the artifacts, especially the architecture, to call to the ghosts within.

After the louts, I ride the trolley back out to Mezaparks, weary enough of the present. I walk there, too, in the green suburb, a place very like the one where I grew up, if grander. Mezaparks was one of the first garden suburbs ever built, so was itself a harbinger of the future most of my contemporaries were born into. It has a home feel to me that is very different than the ghostly reality of the old towns, a home feel based on simple memory. This is a suburban neighborhood, meant to be green, quiet, and safe, although only two months ago there was a brothel in a house on the next street, and not at all long ago many of these houses were inhabited by ten or twenty families apiece, like the urban warrens described by Dostoyevsky and Dickens. And a half-timbered place a few hundred yards from where I'm staying was notorious during Riga's Russian years when it served as the interrogation house for the KGB.

And if you know where to look, I'm told, you can still see the remains of the rail line that served a small concentration camp built in Mezaparks during the Nazi occupation. Architecture won't save us from history.

So how do we choose where we travel? How do I choose? I often think of the poet H.D. in this regard, remembering these lines from her *Trilogy*:

> I go where I love and where I am loved,
> …
> I go to the things I love
> with no thought of duty or pity;
>
> I go where I belong, inexorably…

Ah, how I admire these lines, how I envy their certainty! I think they are as good a formulation of what I intend by traveling as any I've seen (in spite of the fact that H.D. is writing about travel here obliquely, if at all). Still, H.D.'s lines suggest the eros of traveling, that the activity is bound up deep down with love, and they insist on the implacable seriousness of going, on the seriousness of life, however much comedy there is to endure. Comedy is not the same thing as frivolousness, after all. And yet, I don't know what I'll find until I get there, and often enough traveling I don't find "the things I love." Too often my ghostly selves, which might help me escape, a little, being time-bound, and to such a time, simply fail to materialize, and I find myself walking down dusty roads at world's end trying to reconstruct just how I got there.

In Riga, I go shopping for a souvenir, for something small to attach a memory to, for a gift. In the Baltics, such a thing is likely to be amber. I look, I ask questions. The colors of amber, honey, cognac, green, black, and white. The salesgirls point out the occlusions, bits of fern or the wing of a small insect, things caught out of time. In a gemstone occlusions count as a fault, but in amber they add value. They seem to suspend time, and for this the traveler is expected to pay. But I find the equation a little too easy, and we never make anything our own by a simple purchase. The world is a harder, more exacting place than that. So I ask questions, try to know something. Anything I'm at all interested in I touch, getting a feel for amber. Although I like the black amber and the pieces with a dark, reddish hue, it's the white amber that speaks to me with the most gravity. White amber is oldest, the salesgirls tell me, very primly, not old themselves at all. Although they can't explain it, the years in the end press the clarity out of amber, and then what you have is white amber, opaque, not white so much as a marbled yellow, a little honey or bitter lemon stirred into milk. And any moss or moth that might be in it stays hidden, as if behind fog. This appeals to me as the better, the truer story, the way clarity is lost with age, in history, in our own lives. The whiteness. Already I can feel the page going blank under my hand.

In H.D.'s *Trilogy*, birds are the great travelers, and want to be time travelers, too. But like the rest of us, however clearly lost worlds speak to them, the birds must fly the atmospheres of their own time. H.D. imagines her migrants,

> who still (they say) hover
> over the lost island, Atlantis,
>
> seeking what we once knew...

Is it an island under the waves we seek? And if so, what is there to hope?
H.D.'s birds "seek but find no rest/ till they drop," in freefall, from the
sky.

> [W]hat if the islands are lost? what if the waters
> cover the Hesperides? they would rather remember—
>
> remember the golden apple-trees;
> O, do not pity them, as you watch them drop one by one,
>
> for they fall exhausted, numb, blind
> but in certain ecstasy,
>
> for theirs is the hunger
> for Paradise.

(2007)

WAITING FOR THE BOMBS

::

Being Big

Late September 2001
Chiang Mai to Louang Phabang

The plane is small, and operated by less-than-reliable Lao Aviation, but convincingly shiny, and I climb the aluminum stairs off the tarmac confident, grateful as the next guy to be avoiding a bus. But I am one of the stragglers, and I'm hardly in my seat before the stewardesses are calling for seatbelts. The plane begins to taxi, taking aim out of the flat, Chiang Mai valley at the green mountains of Laos to the east. In a flying-trance, it takes me a long moment to realize that the stewardess standing in the aisle is speaking not to the passengers at large but to me in particular. Please, she's saying, this way. And as the airplane picks up speed she leads me from the rear of the plane, up the aisle, to the front, the very front, To balance the airplane, she explains.

Oh.

The nose of the plane tips up, but not too far up, and we're airborne. I feel like I've made an important contribution to air safety.

Over my shoulder, I see a planeload of Thais, small, neat people, and I have to acknowledge the simple efficiency of moving me rather than three or four of them. But that's an exaggeration, surely, two slim Thai to one of me? Not that I'm that large. At home, in West Virginia, my six feet, two hundred, hardly stands out, but since I've been in Southeast Asia—less than two weeks—I have begun to feel large, swollen, shapeless and shambling. Lumpy. The word galoot rollicks into consciousness and sits down. I feel like I've taken some drug and woken up in the mind of anorexia. Food looks less good. I pass on the in-flight snack.

Out the window, the jagged hills of Laos glow an emerald green through the patchy clouds. Soon, the Mekong River snakes into view, brown and rolling here at the end of the rainy season. We begin our descent, Louang Phabang only minutes away.

I think of Delta B. Horne, back in Morgantown, who after September 11 no doubt entertained grave doubts about the wisdom of my traveling this fall. She emailed me she had dreamed we were on an airplane, and everything was okay, except we were all ghosts. Only that.

I look up. The seams of the cabin have started to smoke, but it's not smoke, more like the fog that rises off a cooler of dry ice when the lid's opened. The molding around the oblong windows pours with it, wreathing the view. But we are seasoned travelers, no one panics, even when the seams overhead start to rain down water on us. The mood is festive. One intrepid traveler has his camera out and is considering a picture. Probably he'd like to stand in the aisle, a man in a cloud on a plane, while someone else took his picture, but the seatbelt light is on. So he snaps and grins.

The red tile roofs of Louang Phabang are clearly visible now, the town situated like a miniature Pittsburgh on a narrow peninsula between the Nam Khan on one side and the swirling eddies of the Mekong on the other.

::

Waiting for the Bombs

Late September/early October 2001
Louang Phabang

The first gong resonates like it's in my room, and I'm awake, the silence of 4:00 a.m. still thick behind the single ringing, the air black and liquid. I can almost see the sound vibrating out, waves on a disturbed night lake. It's the monks. Their day has begun. Begins with percussion. There are monasteries (*wats*) all over town, three within a hundred yards of my room in Villa Xiang Moane, itself named after the sweet sound of the big drum in the monastery compound just across the street. Monasteries dot the landscape across the Mekong, across the Nam Khan; one sits on top of Phou Si, the holy hill. There are at least twenty, maybe thirty monasteries within earshot of my bed in the Xiang Moane. Every monastery has a big drum housed in its own building, and soon a monk is standing before it, a soft hammer in hand, pounding morning from the drum's taut hide. And gongs, and cymbals, and old car wheels hung and struck with two feet of rebar, and teak logs, hollowed out, made sonorous, hung and struck.

I feel like my bed is sitting on the strings of a gigantic, prepared piano. Every monastery its own ensemble, playing together, but each on its own, playing alone. The whole is not a concert, but not a cacophony either. Every monastery plays and pauses, and plays again. The rhythm, the spatial effects, are like peepers in spring or crickets in fall. Mysterious, organic polyphonies.

I get out of bed to stand at the windows, throw back the shutters. The golden *stupa* atop Phou Si is lit, casts a yellow radiance up into the still starry sky.

For as long as they play I forget and am happy. Fifteen minutes not bereaved, fifteen minutes without anxiety. Fifteen minutes just a man, all ears, in a town awake, listening.

Breakfast at the Scandinavian Bakery. CNN on a TV mounted high on the wall: *Larry King Live*. The Lao girls bring me a mango shake, a croissant, a cup of thick, Lao coffee. I listen. I can't help it. The question: when the bombs will fall, not if. The news scrolls across the bottom of the screen, all bad. Worse than the news though is the rhetoric. Patriotic frenzy. Whatever will be done, must ideological corruption precede it? Can men who hijack airliners and fly them into buildings honestly be characterized as "cowards"? This from the man who, when he got the news, flew in Air Force One to Offutt AFB, in Nebraska? And wasn't it ideology that made those other guys hijackers? The same kind of lies? I finish my coffee and leave Larry King to the generals.

An American traveling so soon after September 11, I am traveling in the wake. Since I've been in Southeast Asia I've been asked to accept condolences, again and again, for the nation, which feels strange. I am, of course, sorry, too.

One of the good things about being American is that at home I don't have to feel American very often. That layer of identity drops out; for weeks at a time it never occurs to me to think of myself as an American. Traveling abroad, of course, the world insists, asks, Where are you from? In Southeast Asia, this question is asked all day, every day. And now, I'm sorry, and that thin shell of my identity that is national, accepts the condolences, Thank you.

In old Louang Phabang, the main streets are lined with shop houses. There are a few colonial mansions now put to new uses, and beyond that, in the alleys or away from the center, the distinctive stilt houses of the people. And monasteries, of course. I take an interest in them all, walking. But I like best to walk in the evening, when the architecture begins to soften in the darkness, when the monks are in their *sims*, chanting. I might walk the whole town, listening to the chanting swell up as I get close and fade after I walk by. Or perhaps sit on a curbstone or a stone stair, listening, or stand at a gate, looking at the rows of kneeling figures, shaved heads, orange robes. Here there is no before or after, just again, the chants taken up, devotion again. But it's not all seriousness. Some of the monks are only boys, and a serious demeanor at times fails them. One boy will lean and whisper and another's face will light in a wicked grin. Being a monk in Laos isn't only the decision of a lifetime, but a rite of passage that almost all boys undergo, to "ripen" into men.

Another day I climb Phou Si at day's end, leaving my black, rental bike at the bottom of the serpent (*naga*) stairs. Up, through trees, to the golden *stupa*, That Chomsi, where the sun catches last in Louang Phabang. Like much of the religious architecture in Laos, it looks better at a distance, but the voice of a monk chanting saturates the air, his voice filling the vowels with yearning, and I am happy to be here.

The terrace in front of the *stupa* is decorated, flowers in planters made from the tail sections of American bombs, fins serving as feet to support cases now full of dirt. I've seen a few others around town. Reminders. The map of unexploded bombs in Laos from the Vietnam

War is pretty much a map of Laos. Many of these bombs were not even dropped on targets, but just dumped before the bombers returned to their bases. These bombs are still falling, thirty years on. UXO, "unexploded ordinance," kills or maims on average two hundred Lao a year.

What we do keeps going after it leaves our hand, beyond what we intend, sometimes with dire consequences in a future we cannot know.

Another day I visit the Royal Palace Museum; most of my attention goes to the building and not much to the collection. But near the exit, in a display of diplomatic gifts, I see a boomerang, from Australia, of course. A caution. And from Richard Nixon, who also gave many of the bombs, a little clutch of moon rocks.

For days the quiet citizens of Louang Phabang have been preparing for Lai Heua Fai, a moveable feast that falls on the full moon at the end of the rainy season. Celebrated widely in Laos, it falls on a different moon in different places, depending on the timing of the monsoon in that locale. It's the October moon this year in Louang Phabang, tonight. The floats that have been going up all over town will be marched along the main drag to Wat Xiang Thong, then carried down on the great stairs to the Mekong and launched into the fast-flowing river.

Made of split bamboo, colored tissue paper, and glue, fanciful as floats are, every one blazes with candles or spirit lamps. To give thanks, to celebrate the end of the Buddhist Rains Retreat, and to pay homage to the river-dwelling *nagas*. The big floats, twenty feet long and more, are carried by a crowd; they are central to the public festival, but there is a private piety as well. Seemingly the whole town, one person at a time, carries a small offering down to the Mekong or the Nam Khan, to dismiss all that is dark in living, sin and disease, fear and hard luck. Most of these offerings are small rafts made from a banana leaf, cleverly folded into the shape of a lotus blossom. The size of a full-brimmed hat, they are charged with flowers, most with marigolds, yellow and orange, a stick of incense, and a candle.

Before the big floats arrive, I join the crowd descending to the river, serious and light-hearted, and set my offering on the dark water, the incense smoking, the candle lit, a little foil pinwheel spinning in the breeze. I ask that my sorrows be eased and set my little boat to float on the stream.

Only then do I see a darker darkness on the river, long boats, and in them men who, when a candle bobs within reach, cup the flame with a hand and blow it out. My candle! My little pinwheel must now spin the breeze unlit in the watery dark.

But some get by the boats and float the eddies along the shore; others get into the current and go. And still others float down from somewhere upstream, way out, in the middle of the river, racing along.

After I've watched the parade of floats, been carried along by the crowd, after I've listened to the monks at Wat Xiang Thong, I make my way back to the river, downstream, another stair, the same river, the same pious offerings. Again I carry a float down to the water, this one for Delta B., hand it to a boy in a boat who hands it to another, on out to the stern, where the last boy sets it directly in a fast current tongue. For a second, it resists the pull of the river, heels, then it's off, the small yellow flame illuminating the marigolds, and higher up, the dim orange tip of the smoking incense. I watch it ride clear out of sight.

Then the news that the bombs are falling. Each one wrapped in words, in ideology. Wrapped by "us," wrapped by "them," but exploding nonetheless

31

in a real world where real people live and die. And some won't explode, will be added to Afghanistan's already crowded map of UXO.

The effect of these bombs too will ramify in ways we can't foresee. They are both the boomerang coming back from the hand of Al-Qaida and a new one thrown.

::

The Burden

Mid-November 2001
Danang to Hoi An, Vietnam

Motorcycles and bikes, trucks and cars, walkers, all crowd the road from Danang, a narrow road at that. My taxi goes by starts and stops, horn blaring—it is the custom of the road. I look at the people, so young. Few of them would have been born during the Vietnam War, called the American War here. Schoolgirls all in white, in *ao dai*, a long slit jumper over long pants, pedal along in twos and threes, talking and laughing, as schoolgirls do. Some of them hold the front panel of their *ao dai* in one hand, pinned to the handlebars, to keep it out of the chain, letting the back panel stream behind. Boys, some of them in school uniforms, too, others rioting as best they can or working as they must.

Danang to Hoi An is not far, but the trip consumes the better part of an hour. The taxi man drives carefully. We chatter as we go, until he, too, asks me where I'm from. The U.S., I say. Ah, America, he responds, I'm sorry. But I can tell it's not the sorry of condolences. Sorry? I ask, suddenly glum. Because of the war.

Yes.

So many of my people died. Yes, I know. And then I find myself offering apologies for my country.

I am uneasy. I am a man for whom all identities feel a little assumed, and national identity most of all. I have spent a lifetime in opposition. But I find I cannot deny all responsibility. It hasn't been my country right or wrong; I've made free with dissent and, if called, would not have gone. But however tenuous my American identity feels at home, here, I cannot say, Not me. I say, I'm sorry.

Perhaps because the country has a claim I have bridled all my life at ideological attempts to co-opt it, to make it mean a duty to subscribe, to put aside moral judgment and reason. Better to hate all flag waving, all ideological imperatives. I refuse to jump when our leaders say, You're either for us or against us, as they have said again recently. That is how evil speaks; I know the voice, the words.

::

The Beautiful Place

Mid to late November 2001
Hoi An

My room in Hoi An, long and narrow and overlooking Tran Phu, is on the second story of a one-hundred-fifty-year-old shop house, now the Vinh Hung Hotel. The room is dark but soothing. Built post and beam, the main uprights are peeled teak logs; the walls and ceiling are paneled with pieced teak as well. From age or stain the wood has turned almost black. The antique furniture, except for a couple of small wicker chairs, is the same deep purple. There are two beds, an enormous four poster hung with a white mosquito net on a frame with bats carved in the apron, and a smaller bed, in which I will actually sleep, a mosquito net tied up like a great white acorn hanging over it.

The room appeals to me. Like the best vernacular housing, the aesthetic feels derived from use, from centuries of responding to locale and tradition. Here, traditions. Hoi An shop houses have roots in Chinese, Japanese, Vietnamese, and, latterly, French Colonial architecture. Most of the buildings were built by merchants who lived and traded under the same roof. So the front room on the first floor opens convincingly to the street but can be closed up, made domestic. The buildings have public and private identities.

Many of the old houses in Hoi An, however, are now all public. House museums, or they've been converted to restaurants or hotels. I can walk in what were private rooms, and do. I go in everywhere I can, spying out variations and inspired designs. But most of what appeals to me is common: deep, two-story townhouses, a street in front, a street behind. The shop in front, with living quarters above, then a closed garden open to the sky and built against a common wall, balconies on three sides, then another two-story structure, then a garden in the back, then the back gate in a wall. These are townhouses, constructed with buildings adjoining on either side, but they are full of light. The closed garden and the back garden create great plinths of light, and the communicating doors and interior windows allow the light to stand thick and blue in every room. Except for the floors on the ground, originally slate, these houses are all wood inside, floors, walls, ceilings. This gives the interiors a profound visual harmony, a rare organic integrity.

Hoi An is a wet place. It rains, it floods, and often it's hot and humid. The shop houses are built for water, made of teak, and there are removable grates in the floors on the second story, with block and tackle hanging above them from the ceiling, so that when the floodwaters come, and they do regularly, furniture and merchandise can quickly be hoisted to safety.

The river rises a little while I'm in town; the remnants of Typhoon Lingling have swollen the Thu Bon so that on a high tide it rises over the river wall and floods Bach Dang, where the boats are tied up. I walk there at night, not suspecting, and am surprised to see the river in the town, the boats, well down by day, now looking ready to float into the lantern-lit streets.

Old Hoi An must be about the same size as Louang Phabang, and here, as there, I walk myself to exhaustion, looking. In love with the maroon wood and the faded, pastel stucco, I think of the town as unbombed and lucky now for the years of poverty that kept it from the wrecking ball (the bomb of progress).

In the evenings I wash the road dust from my feet, my face caked and hair thick with it. My room in the shop house pleases me; I'm able to continue looking at old Hoi An right into bed. But when I shower I find I can't stand up. The tub has been raised six inches to accommodate the plumbing and that puts the top of my head two or three inches into the ceiling. I hunch, use the soap, getting as clean as I can.

::

Shiva

Late November 2001
My Son

I travel out of Hoi An on a rainy day, to see the Cham ruins at My Son Sanctuary. Bombed, most definitely bombed. The Cham civilization flowered in the region for around ten centuries. The Hindu statuary, here and at the Cham museum in Danang, is sometimes stiff, then again, sometimes an artist with a gift quickened the stone, and a lithe girl dances still, and Shiva wears a knowing smile.

Brick temples once crowded the precincts at My Son in several clusters. French archaeologists, around the turn into the twentieth century, catalogued some seventy buildings, and that centuries after this city, sacred to the Cham, was sacked by ethnic Vietnamese. But at My Son now very few buildings are still standing. I overhear a guide explaining how American B-52s reduced much of what was here to bricks in 1969. The account is less bitter than I expect; the guide seems to lay at least half the blame on the Viet Cong, who took shelter in the ruins, who chose to fight here. I finger a stele covered in the intricate script of sacred Pali, pocked by M-16s, and think of the Taliban's destruction of the Buddhist statues at Bamiyan in March with tank and rocket fire. How even before September 11 that act had turned back on the Taliban. Indeed, in Southeast Asia, the Buddhists I've talked to seem to regard those shots as the first proof of the Taliban's ideological madness, of a karma that would lead to retribution.

Late one afternoon, I ask about another of the side trips on offer from Hoi An, to My Lai. I gaze into the face of the woman at the counter at the Vinh Hung and see a stricken look pass through her features, a wave of grief. I feel I should go, face the worst, the most shameful day of the Vietnam War, but I find I can't. What I know already suddenly seems quite enough, as much as I can bear. I don't need to see that tremor pass through another face.

So I walk down Tran Phu toward the market and drop into an unnamed café full of older Vietnamese men who welcome me to their number with a nod. I order white coffee and sit in one of the low, maroon, resin chairs. It's very small, a size sold for children in America. The coffee comes and I relax out of being American into common humanity. But when I get up to leave, the chair sticks to my hips, and I have to pry it off with both hands.

::

Old Quarter

Early December 2001
Hanoi

I've come back to Hanoi, after an absence. In Hué, I watched the video on CNN, truckloads of Taliban fighters racing down dirt roads in Afghanistan to join the Northern Alliance, pledging themselves anew, ready to fight those remaining loyal to the Taliban cause. Some people just like a good scuffle, maybe.

But ideology creates a need for ideology, to carry slogans in place of a conscience or independent judgment, any flag to march under. And I don't mean just soldiers. The flags of the world's ideological tribes have been breeding. Everywhere it seems people are identifying with more restrictive definitions of what it means to be them and denying that imagination, love, or tolerance could ever allow anybody not them to understand them. Surely this is globalization's twin? A way to resist the forces that would make us all alike?

Even in Hanoi, the capital and a surging, modern city, you cannot walk at all without meeting a Vietnamese woman carrying some load on a stick, a shoulder pole with wicker pans hanging from either end. They embody the traditional figure of justice; they carry the scales. And justice lies in the balance of the two pans.

There has been a lot of talk about justice recently, justice for the terrorists on board the jetliners on September 11, for bin Laden and Al-Qaida, for the Taliban and anyone else supporting "them." As if justice in a case like this were possible. But it's all pretty words and not what's wanted, not at all. What "we" want is bloodier than that. The truer word is retribution, which means, at root, payback. I'm not saying we shouldn't have it. I am saying for our own sake we should call the things we want by their real names. And if what we hope to get, beyond the blood, is deterrence, we should acknowledge that deterrence shares its root with terror. To terrorize "them" so they won't terrorize "us."

There is little justice in bombs, which fall more like the proverbial rain, on the just and the unjust alike.

I sit eating persimmons and a mango with an acquaintance in a Hanoi coffee shop just down the block from what remains of the "Hanoi Hilton." The coffee is good, the conversation pointed. David, an American living in the French Quarter, refuses to answer America to the question, Where are you from? He answers, I'm Jewish. He believes he has made the break, gotten free of national identity altogether. As I have not. While we talk, two women with shoulder poles and conical, straw hats pass each other on the sidewalk in front of the café, going opposite directions, each selling the same array of vegetables, and for a moment I can't speak, just shake my head. I register this small scene as a rebuke to even pointed conversation. For a second what futility means is right there. And perseverance, because the women dip their hats only a little and keep on, undaunted.

In Hanoi there is little to remind me of the Vietnam War, though we bombed here, too, of course; the infamous "Christmas Bombing" ordered by Nixon at the end of 1972 killed some thirteen hundred Vietnamese. I remember those days, hearing how the Vietnamese didn't value life the way "we" did, which somehow meant that our less than sixty thousand dead seemed more important than their three to five million. Those were the days, the upside down days, when "the best" agreed to go to Vietnam to fight and "the worst" said *no*. Love-it-or-leave-it days. And even now there is a great outcry about the reception "the best" got when they came home, and they did suffer and yes they needed all the help they could get to live in America again. I don't begrudge them. They were only boys. But they hadn't made the best decision to go. And it's funny how the patriots' cynical story about those who resisted carried the day: how just everybody against moved directly from protest marches to corporate boardrooms. As if those who found themselves vilified when they stood against the war came away unscathed, as if listening to the lies shoveled out of Washington didn't make them forever doubters.

And doubters are forever ill at ease, always estranged. No monument for speaking out against the ideologues. No one to winnow the bums on skid row and say this one lost heart, lost the ability to believe, the ability to take part. No. At home, too, people were wasted, people who believed they lived in a country where freedom should be honored not only in the abstract but on the street.

I grow old, and am angry still.

And I wonder about the cheap America of the patriots these days, about those who believe the public good is best served by private greed. Buy something, anything, do it for America. Shopping, on eagles' wings…

I go shopping, too. Wandering the 36 Streets of Hanoi's Old Quarter, the city's mercantile district. Here, commerce is face to face, and it doesn't take long to get to know shopkeepers. Or to get known. You're recognized on your second visit, because it's a small shop and the same people are there everyday, nothing like a Walmart. The Old Quarter, a horseshoe-shaped square kilometer tucked between the Red River, The Citadel, and Hoan Kiem Lake, used to stand within walls, and the layout of the streets still reflects the compression of its former fixed limits. The streets teem, alive with buying and selling and living at a pitch. I fear that, like Allen Ginsberg in that "Supermarket in California," I am shopping for images—one of my derelictions, one of the ways I fail to be fully human. But I try to make contact, and it's easy to forget this is Vietnam, because in spite of the superficial differences, the goose blood soup and the weasel coffee, the stonecutters pounding out tombstones in the street and the banyon trees, the street life feels profoundly familiar. Human.

I'm staying in a modest hotel on Ma May, on the riverside of the quarter. The narrow street is in constant motion, cyclos and taxis, bicycles and street hawkers, motorbikes and pedestrians. It's difficult to cross over to the other side. And yet, almost every night I see a man crawl up Ma May; paralyzed from the waist down, he drags himself along with his elbows, right up the middle of the street, a child with a begging bucket following in his wake. The traffic surges around him, not oblivious but not overly solicitous, either. He has a place. Give some money to the child. Show a little compassion.

I go walking, and walking I have become smaller. Eating less, I have become fit on the road. From the first notch in my belt to the last, my pants now blooming around me. A healthy change, physically, and a long way from anorexia, I know. But perhaps metaphorically telling. Thinking myself big, I have made myself smaller. A metaphor for ideology. Not as good a metaphor as anorexia, the real thing, the girls so thin still clinging to the idea that they are big. Thinking big their sickness. Thin to die for. Like *jihad*, like dominos. To kill for.

On my last day in Hanoi, I drop into the Café Pho Co on Hang Gai. From the street, it looks new, a shop full of cheap goods for tourists, but there is a hallway on the right that opens into the garden of what turns out to be an ancient shop house very like the ones in Hoi An. Café Pho Co is in the garden; it's an improbably serene place, just that short hallway away from the loud rush of Hang Gai. There are only a few tables, and a middle-aged Vietnamese businessman gestures that I should share his rather than wait. We exchange nods and settle into the welcoming hush of the garden. When the waitress comes round I order a *ca phe trung*, a delicious concoction whipped out of a shot of strong coffee, sugar, and a raw egg. Fattening, no doubt.

I have been months away and am ready to go home to my small town on a river, home to Delta B. My welcome will be private, domestic. We will resume. Suddenly it will be winter in "the lost America of love." We'll take the dog, Worty, for walks in the graveyard when it fills with snow. We'll talk and laugh and let the bombs fall out of hearing. I remember George Oppen's *Of Being Numerous*, published during the Vietnam War, his judgment on those who "develop Argument / in order to speak," that "they become unreal, unreal, life / loses solidity," and his conclusion that

> one may honorably keep
>
> His distance
> If he can.

And I hope I can.

The waitress brings the *ca phe trung*, and I eat it with a spoon. When I set the mug down I see my tablemate has asked the waitress for a second teacup, one for me, to share the pot of green tea that sits on the stone slab between us. He pours and nods. I nod, too.

(2002)

JUDITH AND HAROLD

::

March 2004

We had suffered one of those sudden dawns you get flying east before our flight landed in Munich. Heads full of siren darkness, we wobbled through the sun-flooded terminal wishing for shades. The connecting flight to Florence arced over the Alps—so many—too black to see below the snowline and too bright to look at above. There are the Alps, I said to myself, because I am always quoting. I wanted to take my whole head into Photoshop and tone down the contrast.

When our taxi turned into the narrow streets of old Florence, the shadows felt welcome as a balm, soothing. Bleary-eyed, we'd still noticed the great banners hung along the route in from the airport announcing a Botticelli and Filippino Lippi exhibit at the Palazzo Strozzi: "Passion and Grace in Fifteenth Century Florentine Painting." The banners featured a beautiful head chopped from Botticelli's *Pallas and the Centaur* and blown up large. Still, our hearts did not leap up and not only because we were tired. We had come to Italy for the paintings, yes, but for early work, for what Delta called the pennyheads, more for Giotto and Simoni

Martini than their heirs. We thought we had less appetite for Botticelli, jaundiced perhaps by the fame of his *Primavera* and *Birth of Venus*, big paintings but just plain silly in our view. Me and Delta, we got your opinions, no doubt about that.

However, we had no sooner taken up the strolling life in Florence, a town singularly well-suited to aimless wandering, then we bumped smack into the Palazzo Strozzi. "Well, we're here," I said, and without discussing it we sauntered under the stone arcades into the courtyard and climbed up the broad staircase to the exhibit.

I'm the kind of guy forever walking in the out door; so I got sideways of the curators' intent first thing. My head turned as if magnetized to a tiny Botticelli on the wall to my right, *Judith's Return to Bethulia*. Small, the painting invites you up close, and close is intimate. Receptivity dilates in the face of small things; we go a little less defended, want to be tender, and the small looms large in consciousness because of the quality of our attention. I first noticed the effect in poetry, because I am foremost a reader, but it's true of small paintings as well.

I took off my glasses, my face within inches of the picture. I considered Judith's sword, her confident stride, the serene beauty of her bright face. I stood there a long time. Delta appeared, put her head next to mine, and then she was gone. A fast looker. And perhaps Judith just wasn't to her taste.

The subject is biblical, adapted from the apocryphal *Book of Judith*. Finding her town, Bethulia, besieged by an Assyrian army commanded by Holofernes, the rich and beautiful widow Judith decided to take matters into her own hands. She set aside her widow's weeds and donned her showiest stuff, "to entice the eyes of all men who might see her." Then, taking her maid with her, she marched out the city gate and right into the Assyrian camp. There, she wrangled an invitation to the commander's tent, a private party (talk about your mistake on the guest list!). When the smitten Holofernes, overcome with wine, fell down dead drunk, Judith beheaded him, and returned with the severed head to Bethulia, to much rejoicing. She ordered Holofernes's head hung from the parapet of the city wall. When the battle resumed the following morning, the emboldened Bethulian soldiers marched against the disheartened Assyrians, who were routed. And the town was saved.

The tale was well known in Botticelli's time; any depiction of Judith would have called up the entire story. So, in a way, all paintings of Judith mean the same thing, the whole story. Even more abstractly, in Botticelli's day the story of Judith and Holofernes was understood to figure the triumph of virtue over vice, of chastity over lust, and having the necessary pluck to do God's will.

Oddly enough, then, the narrative background turns out not to be so narrative after all. The more familiar the story, the more the element of time is drained out of it. Sequence is suppressed—the end registers in the beginning, the beginning in the end. The whole story is known at once, as if from the side, "and then" hardly matters.

A residue of time does remain, of course. In a painting like *Judith's Return to Bethulia*, time is most present at the point of insertion, where the artist enters the story. Before and after hover around the stilled moment depicted in the painting like two great wings. In this little Botticelli, before Judith returned she had beheaded Holofernes, and after she returned, the Bethulians broke the Assyrian siege. Botticelli suggests both things in the painting itself; Judith looks back where she's come from, the Assyrian tents, and in the background, sketchily drawn, the Bethulian soldiers march out the city gate to engage the mounted barbarians.

Botticelli's decision to focus on Judith's return allows him to portray Judith as serene, allows us to contemplate doing God's will as a matter of simple obedience. The sword strokes, while not denied, take place comfortably off screen. There are plenty of other paintings in the tradition that portray Judith in the very act, her sword quick in the cut in Holofernes's neck, her off hand tangled in his hair.

In Botticelli's little panel, Judith strides left to right across the picture. Looking as if she's hurrying to keep up, her maid Abra follows her closely, carrying the swaddled head of Holofernes in a basket on her own head. That makes three heads close together, and a good deal of the painting's energy derives from their proximity. Botticelli painted Judith turned halfway toward the viewer; her head is tilted back, toward the tents, but her eyes seem to be looking inward, a face remembering. Abra leans forward in her hurry and is seen more directly from the side. Her left foot has just missed stepping on Judith's flowing gown; the elbow of her lifted arm, balancing the basket on her head, extends behind Judith's trailing shoulder. Their heads are drawn within inches of each other. Although they must be walking at the same spanking pace, the speed registers more clearly in Abra's dress, which she has hitched up with her free hand to keep from stumbling. The fabric of her dress has whirled into a vortex at the hem; the wicker bottles looped around her wrist strain at the end of their braided tethers, flying behind. Abra's dusky face stares directly at Judith; it is not a look of unalloyed admiration.

Only the height of the shallow basket separates Holofernes's head from Abra's. Her white headscarf is very like the white cloth wrapped around his head, and the loose ends of both trail dramatically like pennons in the wind. Abra keeps a firm grasp on the basket's rim. Still, Holofernes's head has tipped back; his darkened face is turned up, addresses the morning sky. Holofernes looks more a man peacefully asleep than a man startlingly dead. As if in death he's found his part.

It is Botticelli the painter, concerned with it all, who has chosen to bring their heads so close, and our faces close to theirs. Mistress and maid might just as well have leaned apart and Holofernes's grizzled head been carried in a bag (as it is in the *Book of Judith*). The three heads clustered together at the top of the canvas form an irregular triangle, but their relation does not feel static. Perhaps because Judith looks back, Abra forward, and Holofernes up, the three heads seem caught in a planetary whirl around some unseen star.

I stood looking a long time, and when finally I turned away from *Judith's Return to Bethulia*, it was as a man finished. Full up, I'd be able to look at the rest of the show, but only look. I might have left then and been happy; when the cup's full, why go on pouring?

I found Delta in a room devoted to angels, lost in her own private *tableau vivant*, posing as the archangel Gabriel in front of a Filippino Lippi, an annunciation. Delta looked as if she'd just touched down; her reproduction of the angel's pose in her own quivering body was uncanny. I expected to hear her whisper, "Fear not, Mary…" Another way of knowing, and profound. When Delta sensed my presence behind her she turned her face to mine, radiant, "So wonderful," is what she actually said. I asked her if, when she'd looked at the Botticelli annunciation in the room before, in which the angel has not yet quite landed, if she had managed to hover, looking. Immediately she inclined her head, crossed her arms across her chest, and leaned forward, in the pose of that Gabriel, and I could almost see the lilies on their long stem, the bright wings aloft behind her. But Delta was museum weary, too, and we began to stroll, together, less attentive than before.

Delta's not much of a traveler, and if it hadn't been for the promise of annunciations, she might not have agreed to an Italian journey. Perhaps it was the tiny *Angel of the Annunciation* by Simoni Martini in the National Gallery back in D.C. that convinced her. That Gabriel's odd, but winning, squat pose. The heavy drape of his brocade gown. His face, firm but tender. I don't know how to account for Delta's feeling for these paintings, not religion, anyway. But it's a fact of her particular culture; her anthology of Western painting would be thick with Gabriel and Mary. Perhaps it has to do with the central place of the word in the encounter. The sudden appearance of the angel creates the drama—now there where a moment before he was not. But the angel has come to speak, as a go-between. His words are often painted right there between the angel and the virgin, scrolling out, the duration of his speech included in the stopped time of the painting. The divine arrives riding a word.

We paused in front of Filippino Lippi's *Madonna and Child with Saint John the Baptist and Angels*, a long title for a big tondo depicting the naked Christ held waist high by an impassive Mary. The Babe leans out to pick a nosegay from a shallow bowl of flowers an angel offers to him. A trio of angels kneels and sings. A bit saccharine, no doubt. In the background the boy Baptist, already dressed in those unfashionable hides, bides his time. The angels have their backs to him, do not sing to him, though perhaps he is listening.

"Harold," I whispered into Delta's ear, and she covered her mouth to stifle a snicker, unsuccessfully. I was laughing, too, a private joke.

The joke was puerile, perhaps, but not without occasion. For us, Harold was the name of an ugly baby, and in so many paintings otherwise beautiful the only unlovely thing on view is the little baby Jesus. In the

Filippino Lippi, hanging there, Jesus looks outsize, awkwardly splayed and naked—it's a boy!—and bulbous. A baby so big, you'd think he'd be heavy. But no, to judge by Mary's posture and her mostly open hands, that baby must be weightless. And there seems to be something wrong with his age. Elizabeth's boy, the Baptist, within a half a year of Christ's own age, looks already a rough adolescent. But perhaps the problem lies with John, who needs his skins and cruciform staff to be immediately legible, and therefore can't be a baby, too.

After that, we began to see Harolds everywhere, and, as it turned out, Filippino's baby wasn't all of that Harold compared to some others in the exhibition.

Harold escaped from Raymond Carver's story "Feathers"; that's how he ended up in Florence, famous, camping up all those old-master Madonnas—*Madonna and Harold*, often enough. In Carver's story, Jack and his snide wife, Fran, have been invited to dinner by Jack's friend Bud and his wife, Olla. Before they are even out of the car they are accosted by Olla's "Bird of Paradise," the peacock Joey. *"May-awe!"* That's what Joey says.

Dinner has wound down before Olla can be convinced to bring in the baby, Harold, who has been fussing in his own room. Jack recalls, "Bar none, it was the ugliest baby I'd ever seen. It was so ugly I couldn't say anything." The moment stretched—you've just got to compliment new parents on their baby. "Ah!" Fran says, and, "isn't that some baby." Jack volunteers, "He's a big fellow, isn't he?" But Jack exclaims, telling the story to us, that, "It was so pop-eyed, it was like it was plugged into something." Me and Delta, when we read the story aloud, we laughed so hard we wept. But Carver doesn't invite us to look down on his characters, to laugh at them from a height. I know I identified with all the characters in "Feathers," not excluding the bird. And Delta, she told me how once she'd served a casserole so bad the guests had been stunned into silence, like Fran and Jack, until one of them had thought to remark that the temperature of the dish was, "just about right."

So Harold found a place in our world, in the enlivened air between us, where relationship lives. Joey, too. Indeed, Joey first. We began announcing our returns to the house not with, "I'm home," but with a loud *"may-awe,"* which carried rather better, around corners, up the stairs.

Walking through the Palazzo Strozzi, Harold threatened to take over the show. Botticelli's little tondo, *Virgin and Child with Three Angels*, painted with extreme delicacy, of a beauty luminous and refined, suffered the epithet, *Harold at Table*, a title that pretty much deprived it of all its many virtues.

In the painting, Mary kneels in the foreground, center right, while Christ totters toward her from the left. To keep the baby from taking a first-steps tumble, a small angel walks behind him in a crouch, at the ready. Mary reaches out her right hand to the baby, Christ his left to mom; their fingers are almost touching. Here, it is Mary who is serene, her outsize face benevolent and sure; it's the angels who are looking startled, embarrassed even, their confidence shaken. Perhaps they're chagrined because they've been reduced to domestic help, the one a child-minder, the other two, like maids, pulling open the curtains of an elaborate, outdoor pavilion. More likely, they are abashed by Mary, who though she could hardly be more richly dressed, has pulled a breast out from under her velvet cape and with her left hand presses a stream of milk in a white arc in the direction of Jesus. Which falls well short—as if a milking farmer trying to feed a barn cat had painted the floor of the stall instead.

Harold fails to register that he's missing lunch, but he hardly looks to need it. His body seems to have quite outgrown his head. In this, he does not take after his mother. And the arm he lifts to reach for Mary's hand is just bigger than the other, closer arm, which looks stunted by comparison. But there is nothing stunted about Harold from the belly down. The contrast between head and haunch suggests we are looking at parts of two different babies, almost two different species, along the lines of a centaur, half baby, half pig. What could Botticelli have been thinking? About dinner, some smoky trattoria with ham quarters hanging from the ceiling?

If I hadn't been tired to begin with, and exhausted myself further in the contemplation of Judith, probably my response to Botticelli's portrayal of the Christ child would not have been so flippant. I'd like to think so, to think better of myself than I do.

But how I loved Tobias' little fish, the one he carried shining in a sling when he was confronted on the road by Gabriel, Michael, and Raphael, in Filippino's *The Three Archangels*. The fish looked something like a small sturgeon and wonderfully distinct against Tobias' bright red tunic. And of course, I noticed how the angelic getups in the painting, especially Michael's, bore a striking resemblance to Judith and Abra's outfits when they took the rocky path back to Bethulia. I wondered, momentarily, if Botticelli had dressed Judith like an angel to suggest her role as messenger, as a sartorial sign of her famous pluck. She certainly had, in media-speak, sent a message to the Assyrians.

Judith could easily have slipped in among the twenty angels in Botticelli's *Mystic Nativity* without calling attention to herself. Another party she could have crashed. She was dressed for it, even carried the *de rigueur* olive branch; all the angels at the nativity had one. Though, it's true, Judith wasn't wearing that other to-die-for accessory, wings.

Botticelli wrote a message right on *The Mystic Nativity*, in Greek, and Delta and I were glad the curators provided a translation: "I Sandro made this picture at the conclusion of the year 1500 in the troubles of Italy in the half time after the time according to the 11th [chapter] of Saint John in the second woe of the Apocalypse during the loosing of the devil…" Botticelli's apocalyptic understanding of history, of for him contemporary Italy, unsettled us across five hundred years. The apocalypse, it didn't happen, however many times it was predicted. And I associate Botticelli's kind of interpretation with fundamentalist fanatics, whatever their religion.

(I remember stopping once, climbing up the white rocks of Patmos, at the mouth of the cave where Saint John is reputed to have written his ugly *Revelation*, just wishing he hadn't. Patmos, the place itself should have been revelation enough; perhaps that's why he needed the cave, a dark place for a sick imagination. *Revelation* loosed some demons, that's for sure, and what's especially dispiriting is the sad fact that there have always been many ready to welcome them in, to see through *Revelation* to apocalypse now.)

Into the *Mystic Nativity* itself, Botticelli admits nothing ugly. Even the seven little devils in the foreground are more amusing than terrifying and clearly on the run. Under the thatched roof of a shed, Mary kneels amid the livestock, adoring. To the left, an angel instructs the rapt wise men; to the right, another explains the goings-on to the shepherds. Above, an angelic merry-go-round hangs turning in the sky. A round dance, midair. Right in the middle of everything, getting all the attention, Harold lifts a hand as if in benediction. Too old, too long limbed for a newborn, hair enough to look coifed. That baby's just too big!

Delta and I took a last turn through the exhibition, having a second look at our favorites. Delta spotted Joey, present too, here and there, wherever a showy bird was needed. We puzzled for a moment over Botticelli's *Calumny of Apelles*, meant to warn "the rulers of the earth" to be wary of heeding false council. Although allegorical figures struggle mightily in the painting, contesting the truth, the foreground is strangely empty, plenty of room there for a "Bird of Paradise," if one had been wanted.

We spent a happy week footloose on the cobbled streets of Florence. Delta did her heart-struck Dante-on-seeing-Beatrice pose, with the Ponte Vecchio in the background, as imagined by the Pre-Raphaelite painter Henry Holiday. They had the postcard in Florence and Delta bought about a hundred. I tried to remember Dante's description of the scene in *La Vita Nuova*, of that moment when Beatrice first snubbed him.

We looked at paintings, and between the paintings we walked or drank coffee. I was patient with the many long pauses before the polished windows of shoe stores, and Delta encouraged me to buy every hat I tried on in the Borsalino shop; in the end, I favored a black beaver fedora with a modest brim, but I left it in the store. Delta sniffed out the thrift shops like a truffler, and she bought me a slouchy black and green sports jacket I wore the rest of the trip. That Delta. And considerate? She waited outside while I bought spare parts for my Italian espresso machine back home, a Pavoni, known to believers everywhere as The Chrome Peacock.

Everyday we found pennyheads enough, more than enough. Our dreams filled with sad faces framed in gold. And as if the riches of Florence weren't enough, one day we bused down to Siena, and I fell deep in love with the dense blues of Simone Martini's *Maestà* and the blue ground of the painted-all-over chapel in the Palazzo Publico. Almost a peacock blue. Perhaps that I had begun to attend to the ground as closely as to the figures should have registered as odd, a sign that the mind replete is not a mind discerning. My enthusiasm had become general, was only half a step from intoxication. Perhaps it was Harold who saved me, kept me from descending into a state of total idiocy. That ugly baby turned up everywhere. We joked about *The Daily Harold*. I wondered if Carver's pop-eyed baby could really have competed here in the big leagues. I thought he probably could have. Hadn't Carver's Jack insisted, as if presenting his bona fides, "And I know babies"? I had to take him at his word; even here Harold would have been a player. But why was the baby Jesus so often a Harold?

I began to worry the question. The painters had a problem; I could see that. They wanted to show the God in the baby, not just some pretty baby. Trying to paint that difference must have led them into distortion. The Christ baby could never seem little or unknowing, helpless. He had the big part in the pageant unfolding. His every gesture had to be laden with foreshadowing. Even nursing, he was already struggling up Calvary to the crucifixion. How to paint a baby not a baby, a moment including all of time? How much can the figure of a baby bear? Poor Harold! And I thought the painters' difficulties spoke now to the old questions about the dangers of religious enthusiasm, of mistaking a feeling for divine approval. Which also leads to distortion, a loss of proportion, and worse.

On the bus back from Siena, the March hills of Tuscany flitting by out the dirty windows, I tried to tell Delta what I was thinking about Harold, but she wasn't much interested. Perhaps she was already noodling over her short story, "La Vecchietta in Siena," about LaRue, an old lady finding home unexpectedly in the Campo, the bean-shaped plaza at the heart of the old city.

::

May 2004

Back home, we took up the tasks we'd set aside on a whim to chase after the pennyheads. But the trip, the early Italian spring, held on to us even though our own ashen hills still wore the blasted look of winter, had not yet been illumined with pointed green. I leaned a five by seven postcard of *Judith's Return to Bethulia* against my desk light and communed with it often and some more. Still traveling.

I read that the earliest known owner of the painting, Ridolfo Sirigatti, had given it to Bianca Capello, the second wife of Francesco I, in the sixteenth century, to "adorn a writing desk," and I took that as a warrant. The diminutive scale of the panel, according to the scholars, suggests Botticelli painted it for just such a use, "a private purpose." So at my desk I was sitting in the right pew. Sort of.

Although the intended meaning of the painting was legible, plainly writ, not the beauty of the work, not all its manifest aesthetic perfection inclined me to subscribe. The rhetoric didn't compel me, however much it spoke to a way of thinking about the world that's as contemporary as ever. We, too, live "in the troubles," in the "woe." Judith's confident stride, her supremely clear countenance in the wake of the sword, both attract and repel me. The last thing I would want to do is emulate her kind of certainty about God's good will. There she goes, the olive branch of peace in one hand, the sword in the other. She carries the sword out in front of her, and the dark hedgerow below and behind her looks like the blade's long shadow cast across the field of battle. The conjunction of the twig of olive and the sword suggests hypocrisy or delusion to me, and not only in Judith, but "in the troubles" of our time, too. Judith's kind of certainty frightens me, however well it sells. In certain lights, TV light, it seems like nothing more than the brave face of evil.

Judith and Abra's progress across the stone shelf where they're walking the way back to Bethulia could hardly be more dramatic. We lean in close to the small panel, but the two of them jump out at us, like figures in a pop-up book. They crowd the frame on all sides. One more stride and Judith's trailing foot will be stepping out of the frame at bottom, her peaceful hand and perhaps the tip of her bloody sword will disappear to the right. The white sheet on Holofernes's head, held aloft in the blue haze of morning, presses at the top edge of the panel, and Abra's right foot and swirling dress break the frame stage left. Barely contained, that's how they feel, and the pulse of them, their energy, registers more powerfully because of that. And so much depends on volume! Judith and Abra and Holofernes's head have some, plenty. The stone shelf in the foreground and the imagined Judea stretching out behind them pretty much don't. Botticelli has painted the walking party literally and figuratively upright. The verticals of their striding forms stand out sharply against the wavy horizontal lines of the Palestinian ground. The only strong horizontals on view in Botticelli's depiction of the women are in the ties on the bodices of their dresses and the bolder stroke of Judith's long, blue sword.

The whole of the striking palette deployed by Botticelli in *Judith's Return to Bethulia* serves to push the two women forward, first into the eye, but then on in, until they seem to stride, left to right, across the very ground of the psyche. The sun-emblazoned silks of their dresses glow against the earthy colors of the Palestinian landscape. The clear blues of Judith's dress lift off against the vernal greens of the fields behind her, and the gorgeous oranges of Abra's dress seem to have been distilled from the muddy browns of stone and dirt, curaçao out of potatoes. Botticelli, working his pigments into tempera, chose to radically simplify his palette—blue, orange, green, brown, white, a little yellow. Judith is highlighted in Abra's orange, her hair, the fancy work on her bodice, the half-illuminated fall of her dress. The shadows in the folds of Abra's dress, in the white of her head scarf and the white of the sheet shrouding Holofernes's head, suggest Judith's blue. The dead head of Holofernes is painted in the browns of the earth, with highlights showing here blue, here orange.

However small they would prove if you took a ruler to them, Judith and Abra and the decapitated head of the Assyrian dominate the world of the painting like giants. I have to take the postcard down from where it sits on the gallery of my desk to actually see the soldiers moving, perhaps in loose formation, across the distant fields. They are the little people, Carver's people, and almost lost to view behind the towering figures of the heroic world. Barely sketched, we seem to see right through them to the green and brown of a dirty spring. Their living/dying passes away almost unnoticed.

I slip my thumb over Holofernes's head, covering it completely. I'm surprised, very surprised that the painting should be so diminished. Women overdressed for a stroll. The terrible sword reduced to a garden implement: Judith has cut a sprig of olive with it. Significant looks that don't signify. Some spring morning could-be-anywhere. No story. The agitation of the three heads whirling so close together is relaxed, as if under the influence of Quaalude. And formally, it turns out that to feel resolved the picture requires that brown thumbprint on high. All this is true enough, relative, and polite. The harder thing to admit is that the greater loss, absolute, is the cover up, the hiding of Holofernes's severed head. Judith has not only killed Holofernes, she has beheaded him, and Botticelli exploits the raw power of the image of the severed head in his painting. It's an image that's not dependent on context, on its place in *Judith's Return to Bethulia*. No, it would radiate an authority anywhere. Surely, it's the terrible worrying energy of the image that suggests the act, that raises the arm, the hand that grips the sharp sword. Heads on pikes, on pales, beheading *is not* beyond the pale. It has a past, a history, and a future. The beheadings that have recently splashed across the headlines of our newspapers, how different from Judith's handiwork are they? Weren't they also meant to encourage and terrify? God-sure and God-crazy, the boundary line between them is often broached.

Perhaps Botticelli painted an appraising gaze on Abra's face as a caution, to warn us of the dangers run by the God-sure. At least he claims Judith, the beheader, is of his party. He doesn't insist, as our outraged leaders do now, that the beheader is other, that the act is foreign to our nature. And how can they, how can they refuse the truth about us expressed by a century of blood? History doesn't lead us out of what we are, and to pretend it does is to bind ourselves to the black arts. The real darkness breeds in refusing to admit our own nature. Outrage is not a way of knowing but a way of not knowing. As if our modernity meant we were no longer human! It's always modern times, always has been, and we do well to remember we're everything we ever were, human, the children of dirt.

Commentators on *Judith's Return to Bethulia* often suggest that Botticelli painted Judith still armed with her sword for the sake of legibility, to distinguish her from Salome, the Bible's other lady beheader (if by proxy). Salome, her famous dance. The veils. She must have felt sure of her power, too, cocksure, and her faith was justified. It is the Baptist's head in the dish. Perhaps it's surprising that anyone would think two stories so different should require a sword to keep them apart. But like Salome, Judith knew how to beguile with the body. She arrived at the Assyrian tents dressed to kill, and captivated Holofernes, vulnerable, a man. In Botticelli's great picture, even Abra, seemingly demure in her white headscarf, puts a sensual, leather-booted foot forward and clutches suggestively at her groin. And, it's worrisome, Judith's right breast shines a pale yellow in the morning sun, like the signature in a sapphire, distinctly a star.

Salome has come down to us—well yes!—as perverse. The thing she wanted! If hers was a rhetoric of the body, a seduction by dance, there are other rhetorics far more effective. Propaganda, propaganda dressed as the news. Who could doubt that many the demagogue, hidden under a robe or a suit, wears a necklace of skulls? The masters of war who dial up the bombs are not more evolved than those other men who do it with a sword. They have different orders of power at their disposal, that's all.

Less than two weeks before September 11, 2001, Pope John Paul II, speaking to a group of twelve thousand pilgrims in St. Peter's Square, recommended Judith as a model to Christians, praying that she "might help believers to understand and accept the liberating power of God, who prevails in battle and gives invincible power to those who are faithful to his call." I fear that prayer was heard by the faithful on all sides.

Long after I restored the postcard of *Judith's Return to Bethulia* to its place on the gallery of my desk and turned my attention to other things, I heard a loud *"may-awe"* echo up the stairwell—Delta's homecoming cry—and I jumped up out of my chair and took the stairs down to welcome her. How we live here goes unnoticed in the big world, here at the end of a street in a small town in a poor state. The big stories get here, too, of course, and we know how we're meant to think. We just don't.

(2005)

PUPPET HEADS

::

End 2001

It had something to do with the guy in the funny hat. A white cap, with two tails flying over one ear. Those two tails, white and springy, looking alive, unsettled me. When I turned to look at the man—he was sitting in the chair next to mine in the low light of evening—I couldn't keep my eyes on his face. Those tails distracted me. His wasn't a face, but a face and tails, and the effect was lopsided, uncanny. The man's eyes looked for a moment very knowing, then not, glassy. He tilted his head oddly, which gave his face a cockeyed cast, a little mad, but friendly. As if a puppet had got loose of its master. My impression of the man in the hat, I know, might have had very little to do with how he looked and a great deal to do with my own state of mind at the time. I had been traveling alone for months, and the everyday certainties of settled life had gotten more than a little ragged. And just that afternoon I had walked ten or twelve miles in terrific heat down streets I'd been surprised to find almost deserted. Then I'd eaten dinner at the recommended restaurant, a place so large it could have accommodated hundreds at tables set out in an immense garden under the stars. Not to mention the brightly lit pavilions, where I imagine another night wedding or funeral parties dined convivially. I had sat alone at a table for eight, the only customer in the entire place. Occasionally, a white-shirted waiter had floated through the broken light under the trees. Very occasionally he'd come to my table, carrying a dish or a glass, as if it had been turned up in the kitchen only after a long search. The food had looked leftover, the coffee, when it arrived, only a little brown. I hadn't lingered, and so I had arrived early for the marionettes, where, sitting out front in the cooling air, I met the guy in the funny hat, the traditional white cap of the puppet master as it turned out. That was a year and a half ago, in Mandalay.

I had flown in the evening before to a new airport built far out of town, an airport I hadn't even known existed, so old was the guidebook I'd thumbed through in a secondhand bookstore in Chang Mai, where, standing in an empty aisle, I'd decided to make the trip. The airline flew irregularly into Mandalay, and, as I remember it, only one way. You could fly to Mandalay but not back. Perhaps because of this oddity, the plane, small enough to begin with, was anything but crowded. A few heads peaked over the seatbacks, that was all.

The new airport had been built dark miles from the city. The approach was over a landscape like I had never seen. We came in low, at dusk, the light heavy and golden, as if thick with pollen or dust off a moth's wing. The plane carved a slow arc, banking; out my window, beyond the shining wing, the landscape looked very close, utterly strange yet oddly familiar. Until the plane bounced on the tarmac I saw nothing, nothing at all, to suggest what century we'd been flying through. A patchwork of irrigated fields, flooded or stippled with green shoots of rice, raised dikes lined in red footpaths, animal tracks on the causeways.

The fields flat, and all the land that was flat worked in fields. Like an archipelago, a few small hills floated above the paddies. That's where the people lived, where they had returned to in the evening light, home, the cook fires sending up twists of smoke, signals, we live here. Following the smoke down I could just make out the wood and thatch houses showing brown or sun bleached through a thick, green canopy of trees. The hills were all in trees. Here and there I saw a man or a woman walking. All that green world was fast falling into shadow; even as I watched, the gold mirrors of the flooded fields were darkening down to a pewter gray.

But the aureate light held on the heights, clung to the graceful stupas that capped every hill. Simple, but elegant, a bulb narrowing into a spire, every one of them beginning to glow. Most of them must have been white, washed in lime, a few were gilded, but illuminated in that last light they all shone a dusky gold. What I saw, over that wingtip, felt remembered. As if I'd passed that way before.

Soon enough it was the twenty-first century, and I was clearing customs in a building that seemed to have been built and abandoned that very day. A guard, cradling a machine gun in his arms, nodded off on his stool. Even the passport man looked sleepy, pressing the stamp of my arrival onto a crowded page, waving me in.

And so the next evening I found myself talking to the man in the white cap, then taking a seat in a tiered but narrow theater. I sat close up, hardly anyone was there. Ten of us, at most. A small orchestra playing strange instruments. I can remember very little of the show, almost nothing, except for Hanuman, that divine monkey. What I remember of him is hardly credible, so little did he suggest a marionette. He tumbled crazily on stage, climbed the walls, leaped with a wild energy. Somersaults, flips, and happy, so happy. My eyes filled with tears. Mirth shook me, the tears rolled. I was laughing, a river of light rolling through me, the Hanuman energy, weightless, easy laughter.

Show over, the puppet masters stood revealed on stage, every one of them wearing the queer, white cap of his trade.

The next day I met Tommy.

I'd located the small Indian restaurant I'd heard mentioned at my hotel only after a long search, halfway down a grim alley. Nothing about the place suggested it was a restaurant except the Xeroxed menu, which was old and illegible and more in the way of a gesture that there was food on offer than anything else. After awhile, one of the daughters of the house sat down at my table and suggested what was good or perhaps what was possible. I had it. While I ate, I looked through glass doors at the adjoining antique shop, at all the pretty clutter, and at a man working at a desk in there. Two tiny, dirty rooms.

On a bottom shelf in the backroom I literally unearthed a cache of old puppet heads, the paint mostly off and terribly haunting. I rubbed a little of the dirt from them, the faces emerging as if from internment. They spoke to me, especially one with a bald head, a round-faced fellow with a slightly crazed expression. Although the resemblance was not striking, I felt at once an unexpected and powerful affinity for him. Something in him was also in me. I extracted a small pocketknife from my daypack and began to pick carefully at the fine, dried mud that stoppered his mouth. As I worked the dirt loose his mouth leered up at me, his painted lips parted in an insolent grin. I turned him over, dislodging the dirt from his throat and freeing up the wooden mechanism hidden there. When I turned him back upright, looked into his face as if into a mirror, he surprised me by suddenly sticking out his tongue, a long way out. I laughed, thinking, you're mine.

I bought the lot from Tommy, who owned the restaurant and the shop, and who knows what else, a great deal as it turned out. He became my guide in Mandalay and endeared himself to me by the trouble he took with a three-legged dog he had adopted off the streets. I met him regularly during my stay in the city, and we drove, we hoped, beneath the notice of the generals who seemed to have pressed a good deal of the life out of the people. They had even set themselves against love, as we witnessed one evening driving along the moat road, Mandalay Fort on its great square island just across the water. There we saw a truckload of soldiers surround two lovers who had dared to kiss on a public bench overlooking the moat. Tommy swung his low convertible around a block, and we came around again in time to see the couple roughly pushed into the back of a truck. One year for the boy, Tommy said, two for the girl.

In Rangoon, when I unpacked the puppet heads for another look, peering at them, six in a box like a half dozen eggs, what struck me was the paint, how, worn away, it looked very much like the thanakha-painted cheeks of women I'd seen all over Burma. Thanakha paste is often worn thick in a great smear, but soon flakes away to look like nothing so much as worn paint. The effect is ambiguous enough that I hadn't been able to guess if Burmese women painted their faces to attract or to repel. But in Rangoon, I saw women who clearly wore it for beauty, in intricate patterns, like ghosts of the henna tattoos of India. Once, threading my way down a dangerous broken sidewalk, trying not to stumble into the exposed sewer, I saw a woman whose entire face had been painted in a thanakha mask, a delicate yellow, and the play of that color against the skin of her neck was very beautiful.

My puppet must have looked more like her when his paint was new, before he aged so dreadfully. Of course, I realized, peering into the box, he'd lost his body entirely. All he had was his head, but, in spite of that, he still looked cheeky.

Back home, I impaled the puppet head on a receipt spike and left him, I thought, to gather dust on a bookcase in my study, where, to my surprise, he proved hard to ignore. I often found myself staring blankly over the top of a book at him, not as glassy-eyed as he was, but not getting it, either, the confident mockery, the protruding tongue.

::

Spring 2003

Again, this year, I have gone traveling, hoping by estrangement to shake the sense of things that assails me at home. More war, that too. Maybe it's less strangeness than isolation I put my hope in. To be isolated from the constant dunning of our culture, selling not only things, but belief in an agreed-on world. I try not to be buying, but every moment of inattention brims with small transactions, and I am bought, little by little. So I go away. And even the flight over was strange. On the leg from Los Angeles to Hong Kong almost everyone wore a surgical mask: nose and mouth covered, the very air distrusted. All speech muted, indistinct, lips and tongue concealed, the making of words hidden.

I walked the aisles in the dark plane, studying the faces, the heads, exposed above airline blankets pulled to the chin. People sleeping, I know, but looking very simian, their masks puffed out around their jaws. Like monkeys, but with the energy drained out of them, almost lifeless. Transformed by the very idea of pestilence.

::

Movie

Years ago, I sat in the dark at the movies, though I don't remember where, or who I was with, if anyone. I would have been there because the movie, *The Year of Living Dangerously*, was directed by Peter Weir. At the time, I thought he was a magus, maybe, working in film, and a subversive, because anything that doesn't subscribe subverts. I don't mean politics, though in the end politics, where it's not about force, is all about manipulating the agreed-on world. Not to enlighten, but to control.

I had already noticed that Weir's films take place always at the edge of an agreed-on world, where another reality might make itself known. In *The Last Wave*, for instance, the dreamtime of the Aborigines came to disrupt the linear presumptions of Western time in the mind of the Sydney lawyer David Burton. Repeatedly, Weir had turned his attention to that place where consensus loses its grip in the friction between two worlds. In *The Year of Living Dangerously*, the place is Jakarta. The other world intruding on our Western sense of things takes shape in the shadow puppets, the *wayang kulit* of Indonesia. Two dimensional leather puppets, they are held between the light and a translusent screen. In a scene that estranges, that makes even the most mundane event in the rest of the movie feel uncanny, Billy Kwan, a freelance cameraman, demonstrates how the puppets work to the journalist Guy Hamilton.

Holding the puppet Arjuna to the light, Billy says, "The sacred shadow makes the puppet. Their shadows are souls. The screen is heaven. You must watch their shadows, not the puppets. The right in constant struggle with the left. The forces of light and darkness in endless balance. In the West we want answers to everything. Everything is right or wrong, good or bad. But in the *wayang* no such final conclusions exist."

Sitting in the dark, looking at lit characters on a movie screen, we are invited to see their shadows, their souls. Clearly, the puppets on display in Billy's bungalow correspond to the central characters in the movie, Prince Arjuna to Guy Hamilton, the Princess Srikandi to Jill Bryant, a staffer at the British Embassy, and the dwarf, held to the light by Guy, to Billy himself. Billy sees this, has begun to understand in a *wayang kulit* way. He can, because he is not claimed by any world. Although he carries a Western passport, he is only half of the West, the other half Chinese. Far more estranging, he is a dwarf, almost invisible in the big world.

As if that isn't enough, Weir pushes the character even further into the gap between worlds by casting a woman, Linda Hunt, in the role. Although Hunt plays Billy as a man, her Billy not surprisingly has an androgynous look. What's remarkable about Hunt's performance is the extreme animation she brings to the character of Billy; all the things he's not are turned over to show what he is, the strangeness of being human outside conventional identities, the liquid energy that flows unchecked, invisible, enlivening everyone, all identities, without which the human turns to wood or stone.

Billy holds a puppet between a lamp and the wall, working the horn sticks to make the figure move. "Look at Prince Arjuna," Billy directs Guy, "Krishna says to Arjuna, 'All is clouded by desire, Arjuna, as fire by smoke, as a mirror by dust... It blinds the soul.'" Thus Billy cautions Guy, cautions us, and the warning goes unheeded.

Traveling, I ignored the many cautions of the year, the terror, the war, the plague. In my mind, I had already taken my seat in front of a blank screen, already I was waiting for the *dalang*, the puppet master, to animate his puppets and begin.

::

In Indonesia

In an antique shop on Monkey Forest Road, in Ubud, Bali, I asked to see a shadow puppet on display in the window. In my hands, the puppet seemed to be having difficulty with gravity, or I was, because any tilt away from upright and he leaned on over, his leather body bending and the horn handle, a thin flexible strut, pulling hard to get free of my grip.

The puppet in my hand, like all *wayang kulit* puppets, had a particular identity. And knowing little, I knew enough to recognize Semar, the dwarf, by his round profile and genial aspect. Handle in hand, holding tight, I raised one of Semar's arms, then the other, working the lighter sticks that control the puppet's limbs. Pinned at the shoulder and the elbow, stick attached at the wrist, even in my uninstructed hands the arms proved surprisingly suggestive, the small telling motions of our own arms magnified, made more legible.

This Semar had cast a shadow in the night many times; he was old and perhaps a bit floppy because of it. And aren't we both, I thought, lifting him carefully back into his stand the better to admire him. His face was white, expressive, his lips turned in an amused smile, his head tilted a bit back, as if in light laughter, as if he saw the funny side of things, too. He was dressed in a blue and white swirling sash over a checked loincloth, checked to avert evil. The skin of his body, formerly golden, had worn down to reveal the leather.

Semar's a fat man, but not, I've discovered, entirely a man; he is instead that third thing, man and woman (so the casting of Linda Hunt as Billy was not as odd a choice as it had seemed to me when I first saw *The Year of Living Dangerously*). In some traditions, the *dalang* introduces Semar by glossing his name, explaining that it means vague, but vague only in the sense that Semar evades definition; called a man, he looks like a woman; a woman, he looks like a man. Semar is *kyai lurah*, a secret master and divine, when the spirit is in him. But there, in the antique shop, I was looking at the puppet, not the shadow.

That night I walked in the dark down Jalan Raya to Oka Kartini to see the puppets with the life in them, their shadows vivid on the white scrim Billy called heaven.

::

Show

In the shadow play, one of many in the Pendawa cycle out of the *Mahabarata*, the hero Bima would battle the powerful demon Detya Baka. But before the play could begin, the *dalang* had to conduct the rite of *pasupati*, to call souls into the puppets. The *dalang* is a priest, and *pasupati* not only animates the skin puppets, but confers on the *dalang* the power to control them. Soon the play began, the eternal struggle resumed, first talking, then the fight.

It would be easy to tell the story, but what interests me is how the puppets are changed by *pasupati*, how they show the soul that is in them. Sometimes the *dalang* jabs the handles into one of the banana trunks suspended just below the screen, and the puppets are pressed against it, sharply outlined. Even fixed, speaking, they are not still. An arm, pulled back from the screen, might pulse wildly. And when the *dalang* takes a puppet in hand, we leave this world with its familiar proportions and perspectives. Then a shadow might grow suddenly and fly. Often, the face of a puppet floats up, pressed against the screen, clearly defined, while its body buzzes behind it like the wings of a great bee. Soon we feel the souls the *dalang* has called forth are all there, waiting behind the screen, that they come into focus fast, like a hummingbird, furious with life, will hover suddenly at the window, and then be gone. Now the world up there is all apparitions, the shape of things responding to the beneficent and demonic energies shadowed forth by the *dalang*.

It ought to seem stranger than it does, but the world on the screen corresponds with surprising fidelity to the world we feel around us all the time. People, possessed by anger or by lust, but also by bravery and love, loom up, feel larger. Sometimes even known faces are suddenly transformed, the demon taking over, like Detya Baka, hungry to eat us all. And what do we mean when we say we are angry or in love? We don't have emotions, they have us, animate us, and when they do we dance at the end our sticks, limbs humming.

The *dalang*, priest, puppet master, conductor of the *wayang* gamelan orchestra gathered behind him, gives voice to every shadow that appears on the screen. They speak different languages, according to their station (buffoons might even speak a phrase in English), and every shadow has a distinct voice, in keeping with its character. What the *dalang* must do, think about, seems impossible. But watching *wayang kulit*, sometimes you forget to be thinking, and the shadow world feels real. Then, when the demon Detya Baka, a pulsing frenzy in the air, roars, a guttural bellow, you *know*, you recognize a voice you have only encountered muted or in echoes before. It's possible, then, sitting quietly on a twisty plastic chair in a thin scattering of travelers, to quake in terror.

Or not. Many tourists find in the skin puppets no more than a light entertainment to be giggled through. They are the travelers who never leave home wherever they go, who don't even know their world has an edge. Such tourists seem always to be fingering a camera, preferring the image they can show back home to the less mediated experience they might be having if they'd put the camera down. But maybe half of what is wanted is the very mediation a camera provides: anything, however strange, is reduced to a comforting, tiny image in the viewfinder. Not all photography is defensive in this way; a camera can be used to know rather than defend. But a traveler's camera often keeps a world at bay.

Although they had been asked not to sully what is sacred theater with their cameras, a few tourists, sitting anxiously in their chairs, couldn't help themselves; they aimed, their cameras flashed, and when they flashed the shadows of souls in heaven disappeared entirely, the screen illuminated, white and blank.

In *The Year of Living Dangerously*, too, the Westerners assert their own agreed-on world, living in enclaves or luxury hotels, having dance parties to do the twist. And not only the Westerners; almost all the expatriates refuse to peer over the edge, to walk awhile between worlds. At a diplomatic function attended by people from all around the globe, the guests arrive attired in the native dress of their own lands, living as far as possible as if at home, while outside, Sukarno's reign lurches toward a dangerous end.

In the movie, even those who are paid to see don't; for the journalists, "All is clouded by desire... as a fire by smoke, as a mirror by dust." One looks to the girl prostitutes in "the cemetery," another to his boys, and all of them go blind chasing their ambitions, trying to get the big story back to their own world, tidily wrapped in a neat, journalistic formula. Perhaps Guy—for whom Billy had such hopes—most of all. He is literally blinded, if temporarily, by a blow to the head, requiring him to listen, eyes bandaged, to the roaring nightmare coming on.

After the lights came up, I stepped behind the screen. The *dalang* sat cross-legged directly behind a great oil lamp, the fifteen inch flame that casts the living shadows of the skin puppets still burning. That flame must seem to burn from the *dalang's* own forehead as he sits at his work. His face gleamed with sweat; he nodded, gesturing to his assistants, one on each side, and to the musicians behind them. He was putting the puppets away; now they were just sticks and painted leather, and he showed them no special respect. The puppets clattered softly into their box.

The *dalang* held up a white monkey, Hanuman from the *Ramayana*, not seen tonight, and smiled at my recognition. I tried a question, and the *dalang* dropped his chin; still smiling, shining, he whispered, "No English."

I grinned, undaunted; it's good to get to the end of English, sometimes. Without language the body speaks louder, the face, my face, becomes more expressive. It's that or turn away. He gestured, his hand sweeping around the place where the shadows are made. A dirt floor with the remnants of grass mats for sitting on, the walls block and the whole place lidded by a corrugated sheet. It was close, a cave more than a room. Still sitting, in batik or ikat sarongs, heads bound in a ribbon of cloth fashioned into a cap, they were packing up. The puppets disappeared into the *kotak*, a wooden box, storage, but also a kind of drum often rapped while the show is on. When the *dalang* turned back my way, he smiled again, beatifically, and pulled a business card out of his shirt pocket, holding it out to me:

DALANG I WAYAN DERES

The road back to my room in Ubud revealed a town all shut up. A few things only stayed open late. Here and there a lonely street vendor sold hot snacks out of a cart or off a portable grill that glowed orange in the dark. Ears of corn for grilling neat in their shucks. Satay on bamboo spears, smoking over the coals. Something in a bowl, a small oil lamp swinging on a pole over it.

Walking along, I could hear the judgment of home on the *wayang kulit*. I know no culture is a monolith and certainly not mine, not America's, but the judgment we have to contend with is clear: the shadow puppets are merely things, the *dalang* deluded or faking, the credulous audience fools. This is our trance, and it is deep, a powerful magic in its own right. Skeptical and material, repeated with incantatory regularity, with one hand it creates our world, our science, our marvels, while with the other it sweeps the shadow worlds away.

It's a thin world we live in, however brightly lit. A world of things, better things, maybe, but things. A world with little soul in it, little life even. The very word *soul* is often attended by embarrassment; the shimmering world firing at our fingertips is commonly denied. And if it's not living, it's dead, and oddly enough even the stipulated living often slides into death's kingdom.

Trees are wood, cut down for lumber, planted for shade, or good for nothing. Yesterday in the rice fields I watched as small-hold farmers went tree to tree, making an offering to each and every one. A folded banana leaf, flowers, rice, sprinkled with holy water, a thanksgiving. Yesterday in town and in the fields, all over Bali, the trees received an offering.

But I am thinking not so much about trees as about how our own bodies have become material. Looking for love, or sex, revelers head out to "meat markets." Just a phrase, but not random. The body has become more and more like the meat you might poke at under cellophane at your local supermarket. Our thinking makes it so. Stingy of finding soul out there, we end by not finding it in ourselves, either. Even if it means we understand our own bodies as dead.

Perhaps I am fast becoming a cranky old man, but sober and sedentary as I am, I do not forget that I am animate. The body experienced is a tree of light, pulsing and radiant. The arms, the fingers, neon branches. A crown of consciousness hangs over it all, luminous and large. The body experienced is bigger than the body seen, sometimes much bigger. Fifty years of looking in the mirror and still the same question: who is that? What I see is not what I am.

Children need to be convinced the world is not alive, that the rocking horse has no life in it, that puppets and dolls are no more than what they're made of, that there's nothing in the closet or under the bed. It's nothing, darling, go to sleep. And finally they do, deeply. What's suggestive isn't so much the particulars as the larger fact that children need to be convinced at all. Why? Why do they? Unless the world they live in teems with life, a life they are asked to trade for nothing.

::

Dance

Mornings in Ubud, I sit writing at a small table in the Café Batan Waru, a congenial place where the coffee's served thick and somehow I am encouraged. Every morning I watch as the offerings are renewed, not only at the building's shrines—one at the curb and another behind the bar—but all around the premises. Rice, flowers, fruit, shot glasses of coffee, cigarettes, too, all sprinkled with holy water, incense lit and burning. Simple piety conferring grace.

At night, I'm out to watch the dance.

In Ubud, the gamelan plays and the dancers dance every night. Most nights I have five or six performances to choose from in the town proper or in nearby villages. I might walk to the courtyard at Ubud Palace, or ride on the back of a motorcycle to a temple in Padang Tegal, or in a small bus to a community hall in Peliatan, or take a seat in the offered car to Batuan, but I go out somewhere, every night I'm not promised to *wayang kulit*, to see the dance.

Balinese dances are wonderful and strange, unsettling too, but I want to be unsettled. So I leave behind what I know of dance at home and reach out, trying to understand what gets said in dance here, especially in the dance called Legong. Oh, I'm interested in all the dances and am happy as could be to watch Baris or Gambuh. And what I'm going for isn't always what I get. The other night at Pura Kloncing, after the advertised Kecak, trance dancing began, lit by spirit lamps only. Two tiny girls cast in spells rose up to dance a "dream Legong," their movements synchronized throughout like birds turning together, though they danced with eyes closed.

In the pause that followed, two Kecak dancers lit a bonfire of coconut husks in the temple courtyard. I surmised that soon one of their number would be dancing in the fire. I'm not sure what I expected but not the old man who seemed just to appear out of darkness, trotting randomly around the courtyard, his head wrapped in a rag. He wore the small goatee of a priest and the black-and-white checked loincloth of the Kecak and nothing else. And I wasn't prepared at all for the hobbyhorse, distinctly a hobbyhorse, that he carried around on his shoulder, the horse's head just in front of his, mane and tail streaming down.

An old man, he rode like a boy. He rode right into the fire. Face quiet, he kicked the flaming husks, returning to the fire again and again. Two Kecak dancers appeared with brooms to sweep the coals into a glowing bed while the old man trotted impatiently nearby, then out onto the orange bed, where he stopped and knelt, until both mane and tail burst into flames.

Dance over, the old man sat down abruptly in the temple courtyard. Another priest shook a few drops of water from a flower onto his slumping form, and he seemed to revive, waking slowly to this world. No one else went near him. Well after the crowd had cleared out, the old man was still coming to.

The most commonly performed dance in the repertoire of the Legong is Legong Lasem. It tells the story of the King of Lasem, if very sketchily. The dance on stage merely suggests a tale the audience already knows. The story is no more than a shadowy frame inside of which three girls dance.

In the story, the King of Lasem abducts a beautiful princess while traveling in a forest far from his kingdom, a girl who will not have him. Her brother, a King too, mounts an army to retrieve her. Hearing this, the King of Lasem tells his wife and daughter that he must die. He tells the kidnapped girl, who, unmoved by his plight, again refuses him, the King of Lasem. A bird of ill omen appears, which he drives off, but the King knows the omen is true, and he departs for the battlefield to die.

In the dance, the focus isn't on the story, but on what the story makes it possible to see. The sense of stable character, of identity, that story depends on is everywhere infringed upon in Legong. The two legong dancers (called legongs after the dance) wear the same costume throughout, though their identities in the frame story frequently shift— now the queen, now the king, now the captured princess. Indeed, the two legongs, on stage together, at times both represent the queen. The condong, a palace attendant, does make one costume change, donning small golden wings on her forearms to dance the part of the bird of ill omen. But for most of the condong's performance, and much of the legongs', the dancers don't represent any character in the frame story at all. They just dance.

::

Inside Out

A condong appears in the doorway of the *kori agung* gate at Ubud Palace. She is entering at the door where we meet. Behind that door she's an ordinary town girl. At home, she's getting older. She frets and suffers dreadfully the boredom of long days. But on stage, time surrenders its dominion. The condong is always young. All the dull minutes and hours drop away, while those that register intensely expand, radiate out. Entry, meeting, is electric, so the moment elongates: by the watch it will take the condong nearly five minutes to descend the six stone stairs to the dance floor. She doesn't so much stand in the doorway as hover there, her shadow lifted onto the stone and brick of the great gate behind her. When she has fully entered the floodlit stage, it will be as if she casts no shadow at all.

But still she hovers at the door. Her face is framed by a large and winged golden headdress surmounted by two sprays of frangipani blossoms, each spray tipped with a red hibiscus flower. Standing high above her head, like antennae or soft antlers, they quiver, sensitive to the dancer's smallest motion, and she is always in motion, though much of the dance is carried by movements so small as to be almost imperceptible. As impossibly large and shimmering as her headdress would seem outside the dance, it is only in keeping with the rest of her dress. She's arrayed in layers of gold leaf patterned silk, her skirt and fitted sleeves glow a saturated crimson. Around her neck, she wears a brilliant beaded collar, fringed in scarlet yarn, that extends to the far edge of her shoulders and drops in front of her breasts. Her torso is deeply bound in turn on turn of golden silk. She wears a heavy split stole, worked in gold brocade, which drapes to her knees in front; in back, a great filigreed belt shines. Her upper arms and forearms are clasped by wide buckles, her ears are pierced by heavy conical earrings, and red tipped chains dangle from gold bosses on each side of her face. She shines.

All we see of her skin is face and hands, her feet. Her knees are almost always bent, her back deeply arched, and she twists her arms sinuously. She poses, but the effect is not erotic, doesn't call attention to her in that way at all. We see her face, her hands. A deep vibration starting in her knees keeps even her posing from ever being static. Her fingers are spread—like ours when we hold our hands out, feeling our way, walking in the dark—and vibrating. Each finger hums under a separate volition. She looks at her hands often, as if astonished. Her feet shift from stance to stance but she is never flat-footed. The toes on her planted foot are turned up, while the other foot, perhaps, is pointed directly down, barely touching the ground. Her feet are not still, but pulse, a quiver that registers as a shimmering in all the gold about her. Her body shifts pose to pulsing pose, her crowned face shining over it. The condong turns her head very little, but hers is a face of unearthly animation. She looks out, startled. Her face registers intensely the sheer wonder of being alive, magnifies it, because the lulls between intensities are struck out in the quick shifts between unstill poses, the sudden appearance and disappearance of expressions on her face. Her eyes, wide open, dart side to side in continuous surprise; the whites of her eyes, her eyes snapped shut, are part of the dance. Her chin flicks, left and right, with extreme rapidity, as if she were dancing under a strobe.

Familiar emotions pass through her face, come and go, and come again, every one fully expressed, then gone. Looking, you begin to see what animates them all. It dances, you see it in the dancer, in the dance. It turns the inside out. The gap between what you see and what you feel closes.

Of the twenty-odd Balinese dances I've seen on the stages around Ubud, the Legong is perhaps the least natural. This might at first seem at odds with what I've just been saying, but I'm not suggesting that Legong is unnatural, nor supernatural (words with little if any proper scope). Legong is artificial, made by art.

The art in Legong has roots hidden from me, in the archaic dance Gambuh, certainly, but no doubt running deeper than the best guess of anybody living. I can only see, and then perhaps but a little, what has been achieved.

And dance doesn't only develop from dance. Just as painting influenced poetry in the West, and photography painting, and film all three, Balinese arts talk to each other. The skin puppets of the *wayang kulit* are commonly acknowledged as a major influence on traditional Balinese painting, the Kamisan.

In both, the face is seen from the side; it's a world of characters looking away. *Wayang kulit* and Kamisan are primarily narrative, and because the characters need to be recognizable for the story to be told, exaggeration flourishes. The same cast of characters might appear several times in a

Kamisan painting, each portrayal catching a significant moment in the tale. In this, I suppose, Kamisan is a little like our comics, and, oddly enough, also a little like Legong. In Kamisan, the ground, space, is used to abridge time, to tell story with great economy by moving from one telling incident to the next, while in Legong, the dancers elide time by moving directly from one eloquent expression to the next.

But if in *wayang kulit* and Kamisan portrayal is overwhelmingly in profile, Legong looks straight ahead. Although you often see the dancers from the side, or the back, they are looking forward. In turning, they are far more likely to turn back then around. The forward quality of the dancing contributes to the surprising and counterintuitive conclusion—given the supreme animation of Legong—that there is something of the mask in these faces, or better yet, something of the puppet, and I'm reminded of my Burmese puppet head back at home, waiting to mock my return, that insolent tongue. The Legong dancers, of course, don't stick out their tongues. Indeed, the puppet is suggested a good deal by the very fact that neither the condong nor the legongs ever open their mouths. Part of the eloquence of their faces is the eloquence of the mute, who without words finds another way. And what the Legong dancers turn inside out is what animates words, not words.

The face is painted, a sharp hairline and side curls, extreme eyebrows. The lips large and red. The eyes are picked out with boldly colored shadows, and the whites show as on a face astonished always. Pinned open or snapped shut, they are like puppet eyes. And yet our eyes are expressed in them, our eyes when we find ourselves most startled into life.

The condong descends the stairs. She dances, shimmering, light rippling off her in waves. The gamelan plays, we sit in a spell.

Then the two legongs appear in the *kori agung* gate, very like the condong, not less splendid, indeed a little more. Their gold-flowering silks shine a vivid green. The legongs wear stiff, gold bodices and a single, wide stole in place of the condong's beaded collar and split stole. They too descend the stairs. Three girls together.

We live in the isolated glow of our own animation. Each of us, like evening's last firefly, lives alone in the luminous bell of our own consciousness. We have to imagine that the meadow is full of lights, to imagine what is actually there. It takes an effort in a culture that has plucked the soul out of the body, where we are encouraged to live, literally, in a state of suspended animation. Legong reminds me of that world I cannot see. On stage, the dancers all glow as they dance this life together. And I like to think that it's as a metaphor for our life together that a field of fireflies appeals to us, a starry night, the twinkling of city lights out the window on a long flight home. What we feel then, I think, is nostalgia, not for a home lost, but for a living world.

The condong exits to don her golden wings. The two legongs dance together, then one alone, now the King of Lasem. When the condong enters again she comes as the bird of ill omen. Her little wings attach at the hands, not the shoulders, and she beats them furiously; the air shakes with broken light. She has a message to deliver to the King, to all of us spellbound, who watch. The King knows the omen is for death, and that it's true. Still, he doesn't want it. When the bird attacks, he beats her back. Indeed, the King of Lasem drives her from the stage, wielding with effect a gold and scarlet fan. But still the King must die.

I walk alone into the dark streets of Ubud. A little lighter than before. Not thinking. One after another members of the gamelan buzz quietly by on motorbikes. Then one of the legongs, sidesaddle, slips by on the back of a Honda, her silks darkened now. Then the other one, astride her own bike, her gilded headdress still on, flaring, floats like a dream down Jalan Raya. There and then gone.

(2004)

SELLING

::

It was a cremation but forecast festive, and slow getting going. The body was still inside Ubud Palace and a period of milling around had set in. Folks in the street were getting restive, beginning to burn too in the Balinese sun. The crowd had begun to thicken around shady patches with a view. I was standing in one of the shady spots and not totally proof against the anxiety continual shifting under compression will produce. I had my stone face on. I'd been wearing it since the awful Australian couple had pushed in next to me a few minutes before. They shared that overcooked look certain oily types exhibit when they get old. Too much too-wrinkled tan, and too much of it showing for the occasion, way too much. If they'd have shut up, I might have taken an interest in their grilled looks, but they whined. She did, anyway; his face was contracted into what must have been a habitual sneer, a mask. The woman whispered loudly that the guy next to her kept pushing her and that guy would have been me. As if. I was faintly amused.

But the couple directed their ire on me only in passing; their focus was out there in the sun, had settled on the street hawkers. I'd been watching a bent man myself, who was trying to sell conical hats, like

Vietnamese field hats, but painted in the traditional Kamisan style of Bali. Good looking, and they would cast some shade, but the bent man was having no luck selling them and was looking dejected. He'd looked dejected when he arrived—I'd seen him come and marked at once the legible character of his worn face.

The Australian couple was yammering hard, an outraged commentary on a woman selling sarongs and sashes, Balinese caps, to lightly clad tourists who might want to show a little respect. It registered late that the grilled Australians had shook her off gruffly just before they climbed the steps to where I was standing. The woman selling sarongs hadn't approached me, perhaps because I was already wearing what she was selling, a batik sarong, a proper sash, a funny little hat.

"She's asking a hundred thousand!"

She was, a deprecating smile belying the seriousness of the number. A watcher, I felt chagrined not to have noticed the sarong seller's face before. Sarong sellers were thick on the cobbles of the blocked street in front of the palace, especially around the feet of the great black and gold sarcophagus, a kind of overgrown bull built just to house the dead man when he was given over to the fire. At first glance, the street hawkers all looked the same: wares stacked high and balanced on their heads, arms and shoulders draped with batiks and cheap shimmering stuffs. Except that face.

The sarong seller I had missed fell, if anywhere, a little below average in appearance. Her own sarong was rumpled, and she wore a dingy white T-shirt over it, a T-shirt of the worst sort, awful graphics in faded baby-toy colors disfiguring it. Cheap rubber thongs, pink, I think.

"The nerve! She's shameless, Bob!"

She must have been in her forties, I'm guessing, and forties in the tropics shows a lot of weather. No make-up whatever. But good carriage and clean, even teeth.

A half hour later the Australian couple's censure had not flagged, nor my attention. The sarong seller had made several sales, always the same price, as much as she could get. Which varied, wildly, and I think it was this more than anything that excited the biliousness of the Australians, who, in any case, had been crowded left by late arrivals.

Every transaction ended amicably, I noticed, and that she'd enjoyed sales plural under the circumstances struck me as highly improbable. The goods were not so good, the competition heavy, and the tourists already hardened to being dunned on the street. She sold to people already appropriately dressed. With her face.

The face the sarong seller showed in the pre-cremation crowd was the most expressive I'd ever seen, bar none. I know the bald statement must sound incredible, but it's true. Yes, I've seen anguished faces and faces whitened by mortal dread, faces lit by sudden joy, and nothing that registered in the sarong seller's face was anywhere near so intense. Oddly, I have no idea what, if anything, she was feeling. Hers was a made face, artful, and not at all about extreme feelings. No, her expressiveness shone as pure animation, like a breeze in the wintering leaves of a small beech, like the silver rippling of a stream over small stones. Before any look was fully formed another had begun to replace it in the reaches of her face. Really—I'm only realizing it now—her expressions fell within quite a narrow range! All genial, encouraging, a very light, almost abstract flirtation. But even within so limited a range, the sarong seller never seemed to repeat a look. Perhaps she did. But my impression was that she had independent control over the most minute parts of her face and therefore had a vast repertoire of faces to show. All affecting.

The procession began. The crowd thawed and quite suddenly the bull sarcophagus swept by, bobbing on the flood, a young man tied to its back, holding on for dear life. Then the ceremonial stair and the nine-tiered tower, on which the body and a few members of the family rode, one man holding aloft a stuffed bird of paradise in his free hand. The structures were enormous—the tower maybe sixty feet high—and fixed to heavy frames made of triple-layered giant bamboo. The authorities had taken down the wires across Jalan Raya so the procession could pass, blacking out power all over Ubud. That dead man was carried at a run.

The too-tan Australians elbowed their way out into the crowd in the first wave and were swept away. I never saw them again. A few minutes later, I waded into the current myself and was borne far down the main street of town to Pura Dalem, the Temple of the Dead.

I left the sarong seller's face behind, but even in the jostling and high-spirited race to the burning ground I was thinking about it, seriously charmed. A few days before, I'd read a digression in *Balinese Dance and Drama*, by Walter Spies and Beryl de Zoote, which had casually explained the superior expressiveness of a particular Legong dancer by noting simply that as a child she had been a *dágang*, a seller, in the little carnival of treats that often springs up around a dance performance. Spies and de Zoote—writing about Bali in the '30s—described the selling going on around the dance, the *medágang*, as a virtual "school of deportment, of flirtation and seductive glances." Like everything else in Bali, if then more than now, *medágang* had been elaborated and refined into something like an art. I immediately recognized the sarong seller in Spies and de Zoote's description of *medágang*—sure as I was that what I'd seen on her face could not have been strictly a personal quality, though she must have had extraordinary aptitude. I'd seen the sarong seller's face in fragments in many other Balinese, selling and not. In hers, I think now, I saw *medágang* whole.

At a cremation in Bali, a watcher soon comes to understand there will be time to think, plenty of time. After the body is carried down the ceremonial ramp, out of its nine-tiered tower, and borne in circles around the sarcophagus—and almost dropped to the delight of many but maybe that was show—and closed in the body of the looming bull, after the priest has chanted and blessed the body and the mounded offerings, and the wood has been stacked and soaked in oil, after the fire has been lit and the wife has made as if to join her husband on the pyre, in suttee, and has been ritually restrained, after everything is flames but the head of the great bull, and the guests and the hired help have gathered in the shade to eat and drink, there is time to wonder, hours to consider and reconsider.

Even for a traveler, self-consciousness doesn't press in to ruin things. At a cremation in Bali, tourists are welcomed, even their inanities. They enjoy the rare fortune of a role that doesn't involve spending money. The raucousness of the proceedings is meant to confuse the spirit of the dead man so it won't return to haunt the living. The know-nothing ways of tourists are welcomed, then, as conducive to bedlam. Probably I failed my part, quiet as I am.

I'd been watching and hadn't seen any sign of grief. Even the wife's gesture to suttee had shown clearly as pure theater. She looked tired; that's all. Those most closely bereaved looked occasionally serious, but never stricken, nor even sad. I searched for loss in their faces and didn't find it, nor any sign of strain to suggest the faces they were wearing were put on. How you believe makes death different, it hardly needs saying.

While the fire burned, still under the influence of the sarong seller's *medāgang*, I found myself thinking again about faces, about mine in particular. Curiously enough, it's been one of the great facts of my life. Perhaps your face always is, so in an abstract way I guess I'm talking about you, too. As far back as I can remember, my face at rest has elicited the question, What's wrong? I was as sweet-tempered a male child as you can imagine, but even so in grade school I regularly bore the blame for my misbehaving friends' infractions. My best friend's mother asked that her son be placed in a different class, another forbid me the house. Girls turned skittish under my dark gaze. Smile! I heard it all the time. Cheer up! Injunctions that did not help but made my face stiffen. And, Sell yourself! Advice I always found singularly chilling.

In short, I had no *medāgang*, none at all. And no school to learn it in. No examples of faces rippling under the light breath of sheer animation, so attractive. Perhaps I would have wanted that. Those who sold themselves in the school of my youth struck me as frightening creatures. Faces not animated but contorted into fixed, wooden smiles. To that boy, it seemed a world of hideous, grinning masks. Or morons. A boy with a problem, obviously, and I knew it even then, but knowing didn't solve it. I haven't solved it to this day, nor given up trying; even in middle age I have retained a hopeful sense of becoming.

Once the sarcophagus and all the funerary offerings had burnt away, except the bull's surprisingly elegant neck and confident face, two men with stout poles began to prod the dead man's corpse, tearing the winding cloth off in flaming layers, freeing the body to drop into four wire rings suspended from an inflammable frame.

Even hanging over a roaring pyre, a body burns slowly. This man emerging from his sheets did not hurry. To help him along, the men working the cremation doused him in coconut oil, running it over him out of the hollow end of a wrist-thick length of bamboo, and the flames leapt up, licking and crackling. The crew labored intently—it was hot work—like men tending a great fire in an open hearth.

I sat down on a stone in the flickering shade of an arching palm to wait. There would be time. Perhaps still a little under the sarong seller's spell, I began to mull over an uncanny experience I'd had buying a few nights before. The shadow puppet performance I'd planned for had been canceled, the puppet master detained by religious duties in his own village. At loose ends, I had wandered into a shop on Monkey Forest Road, an antique shop specializing in textiles, ikat mostly. I had been enjoying complete success in resisting the ghostly beauties of ikat, not least because the pieces that most attracted me were old and rare and expensive. It felt safe to look.

The shop girls weren't much help; my questions, as I sorted through the stacks of ikat on display, puzzled them. Soon, they called the manager out of the back room where she'd been sleeping. She entered dressed in flannel pajamas of the floppy sort I'd worn as a boy. Airplanes in the pattern. But she woke up selling, and with the advantage of her

PJs: she'd gotten out of bed to talk to me. She introduced herself as Wiwi Tan, and to my questions, she had answers. She showed me how to tell what was old, what was hand spun, and what not, which blue would prove real indigo. All her instruction was light, her easy banter often broken by laughter, but she was shrewd. Looking over the small ikat pieces I'd picked from the stacks on display, she directed the shop girls to open a trunk of similar, but better pieces, "collected by my father many years ago" in West Timor, where the family had lived for generations. Or so she said, her mobile face flashing a wide smile perhaps ironic.

And the show was on, one haunting thing after another rose up out of her father's trunk. The smell of camphor suffused the room. Even as she sized me up, as she understood what I wanted before I knew myself, she seemed unable to resist a joke, many of them not so funny, ambiguous, slyly aggressive. But she always smiled and laughed, just kidding, always kidding. Her *medāgang*.

Then four pieces remained, spread out on the tables around me, the others folded and put away. I knew I was going to be buying some ikat after all; Wiwi knew, too. The negotiations began. An old traveler, I have my own elaborate stratagems. Very useful when it comes to bargaining, especially, as with ikat, when I have at best a foggy notion about what a fair price might be. How much for these two, for this one, for all four? And delay, just drawing out the dance of buying, selling.

So I was delaying when I pretended to lose interest in the ikat, feigning interest when I began to quiz Wiwi about the primitive West Timor masks displayed here and there on the walls. One did speak to me, its flat oval mouth and long, dark face; the sadness of mortality seemed everywhere worked into the planes and smooth curves of its fixed expression. I lifted it down from the wall, the most familiar fright in the gallery of nightmare faces hanging there.

Wiwi, I asked her, are these the faces you see in bad dreams?

Wondering, I guess, about the cultural conventions of nightmares and if these rude masks somehow manifested that world for her.

No, she said, gesturing at the mask in my hands, her face open, dilating, a smile so lively. No, she said, that mask it looks like you, like your face.

I did not think the resemblance striking. Ah, I said, too stunned to speak. Then I held it up to my face, peering out at a constricted world through the mask's small eyes, considering. I felt a familiar pang, but sharply. Estranged from my own face, estranged from the world. Wiwi grinned, ready to bargain. I was ready, too, but I thought the real deal had already been done.

Sometimes, often, I feel I'm attended by a ghostly double, another fellow, not me, standing just beside me or peering over my shoulder. A gloomy guy, a regular death's head. When I'm alone, I'm alone, but when

I go out, meet someone, he's likely to turn up. As if he prefers company. The oddest thing is that though he's a ghost and a dummy, to other people he's realer than me; he *is* me, to them.

Looking through the mask in Wiwi's shop I felt that other fellow wasn't so much beside me as I was looking out through his eyes, my view constrained, my self hidden. Maybe. But what was true for me was true for Wiwi, too, for everybody: a crowd of dummies, getting together. Wiwi's dummy wasn't a death's head, however, not at all. She was no straight man, that joker.

At the cremation, the living were fading away. The burning grounds had thinned, the sun fire enough to disperse casual observers. The dead man's dummy had charred but was still distinctly with us, taking his time. He had gotten beyond hurry and, perhaps, misunderstandings.

The gap between who we are and what shows on our faces had radically closed for the dead man. There can be no gap when there is only flesh, and soon there would be no flesh, either. Perhaps one of the attractions of the fleshly life is grounded in just this: the luxury of relaxation, of letting the tension go. And in this perhaps the life of the mind is not so very different; forgetting the face relaxes us, too. Still, the big difficulty cannot be overcome. The face is flesh, thoughts, feelings, all the worlds of consciousness, are not. Obviously. Yet about this I must have been confused growing up, thinking I should make manifest what was going on inside me. Integrity demanded it, I felt, but the whole project was futile. The face bears at best a metaphorical relation to consciousness. One thing standing for another, and out of the yawning gap between them rise up the specters, masks, puppets, the painted faces of mimes, the cosmetic arts, the faces of actors, conventional faces, the faces you prepare "to meet the faces that you meet." Most of life is so much signage.

Ana María Uribe walked by, equipped as ever with her video cam. When I greeted her, she stopped to talk, even standing not much taller than me sitting. A singularly intrepid traveler, she had made several trips to Lake Batur by bimo, the small public vans that ply even the most out of the way roads in Bali. She had gotten as far as Trunyan, an animist village there, but hadn't been able to find a boat to ferry her to the graveyard at Kuban, where the villagers of Trunyan exposed their dead in bamboo cages. Something different, not cremation or interment.

Ana said she'd make one last try tomorrow. I admired her, the project wasn't even her own, but a favor for her partner back in Buenos Aires, an artist working with the anthropology of death, its varieties. She had, I gathered, a small reputation as a poet herself. Her father had been one of the leading literati in Argentina in his day. Growing up, Ana's house had been full of South American writers, and once, when she was a girl, her dad had taken her out to lunch with Graham Greene. She wasn't much of a smiler.

Out in the sun, I noticed, the cremation crew was treating the corpse with surprising roughness. They had been exploring his chest cavity with a blackened cane poker, and now one of the workers stood in front of the suspended dead man, banging him hard on the forehead with an enormous, blunt bamboo pole. The force of each strike drove the dead man back and forth, swinging on the iron rings that kept him from falling into the fire.

Ana made a circuit of the pyre, recording. When she returned, she told me she'd managed to get herself invited into Ubud Palace the day before, where she'd been able to film some of the private ceremonies that had preceded the public cremation. The family had permitted it, welcomed her even.

I told her how another year, in Kathmandu, visiting the temple

Pashupatinath, the most sacred site in Hindu Nepal, I'd chanced on a cremation along the Bagmati River. Only Hindus are allowed into the temple proper, and I had walked down through the temple complex alone, chastened just to be there, a tourist. Monkeys frowned from the rooftops. The place was beautiful, yes, but immensely heavy. Literally dreadful. Nothing of Balinese lightness there. I'd crossed the holy Bagmati on a footbridge; downstream, an oval of ashes still smoked on a burning *ghat*. Oppressed, I'd climbed up the hillside away from the channeled river where it ran against the foundations of a temple, up into the white necropolis. When I got far enough away, when my presence felt permitted, I found a place to sit and gazed down to the river, not so much trying to understand as just to feel my way into the dense atmosphere of the place. Not to resist, but to open to it, to the teeming air.

Then I realized that the small figures gathered around something orange at the edge of the Bagmati were preparing to light a fire. The orange streak was a body wrapped in a winding sheet, the brown fringe around it, sticks. Then there was a little yellow fire, which spread; a twist of smoke rose over the river. The living stepped back, except a small child, who rocked back and forth, wailing. He would not be consoled or come away. His long cries echoed through the white stone of the necropolis to where I sat, heartsick, too.

Ana nodded, not so taken with my story. She too had been to Pashupatinath on the Bagmati, and to Varanasi on the Ganges. Perhaps she had traveled too far; so I didn't tell her about my mother, the plain eight-inch-square cardboard box, taped shut.

Ana remarked that she'd be staying to the end, hours more, and I said I didn't think I would be. Even in the palm shade my feet were burning. At one point I had cut through a stretch of low weeds and gotten into something hot, what felt like nettles. Or maybe it was sun poisoning. Either way, patches of small water blisters were now visible between my toes. Was it rude to call attention to my feet? In any case, I soon had my thoughts to myself again.

Before I bought the ikat from Wiwi, she claimed one of the brown pieces, from West Timor, was over a hundred years old. But how can you know that? I'd asked, hoping to learn how to see such textiles a little more clearly. But Wiwi had just thrown up her hands, grinning, and exclaimed, Because my father told me! With that, we made a deal, for the century-old brown piece and one in indigo. After the shop girls prepared the package, Wiwi slipped the wooden mask, my face, in with the ikat. A joker's gift.

And so what if the face is all metaphor, so much signage? We read the signs, after all; it's one of the ways we try to know, one of the ways we try to be known, or to deceive. Hadn't I been confident about what the old Australian's fixed sneer said about his consciousness? Perhaps my problem had always been just that my signage was out of control. No doubt I had created that mask, my face. Not willfully, nor with any art.

My difficulties were in part cultural, a mute protest against the strange migration of identity outside, onto the face, the body. Would it even be possible to go much further into that country? When I was born, the caravans had already been traveling a long time.

About the sarong seller, I wondered why her face, the artful face of *medāgang,* should have so pleased me? Expressive, it didn't express what she was thinking, feeling, but to an extraordinary degree it did show the difference between a live face and a dead one. It helps to have looked at the dead to know how living shows. It is in motion, yes, but not only. Like sunstruck water rippling over stones, it's not wholly transparent.

The afternoon had cooled a little when I got up to leave, and things had quieted down. The dead man looked a little smaller. Odd to say, the space he was hanging in seemed not to be there. He had burnt down to an absolute blackness, dull as ashes. He seemed more of an absence in the flames than a presence there. Looked at in profile, he seemed to have no depth, none, like he'd been cut out of a blackened tin sheet. But his absence had a shape. He'd been suspended chest to the ground, and in the fire his back had arched, his face come up, as if he was looking ahead. An absence in the shape of an angel.

His ashy blackness made me think of the shards of glass my brother Keith and I once smoked over a candle, when we were kids, to view a solar eclipse. That memory came to me old and broken and arrived alone. I have no idea what year that would have been, when we stood side by side on the front lawn to watch the moon swing silently across the face of the sun.

The next night I attended a performance of *gambuh* in Batuan, a village long associated with this archaic dance drama. Ana turned up, too. An old man singing among the bamboo flutes, a high quavering line, quite unhinged me. It seemed pointless to call the performance good. In the van, on the way back to Ubud, I asked Ana if she'd managed to make it all the way to the graveyard at Kuban. She hadn't, nor would she get another chance: she was leaving in the morning for Surabaya in Java, where she'd give up her bimos and start flying, at last, the long way home to Buenos Aires.

She said she'd arrived back at her room from the cremation after midnight and just hadn't been able to face the hard journey to Trunyan still not sure if there would be a boat running to take her on to Kuban. I sympathized, secretly relieved she could be stopped. The woman made me feel my years and easily daunted.

Had the cremation lasted so late? I wondered aloud.

You should have stayed, she observed dryly. Things got interesting after you left. She told me all about it.

After the dead man's flesh had burnt away and his ashes cooled, his bones had been broken up and some of them ground to a fine paste, which the bereaved had applied in a dab to their own foreheads. Then the dead man's remains were gathered up and taken down to the sea at Sanur. The family made the trip with the ashes in a motorcade, Ana, too;

she'd managed to get herself invited to join them in one of the cars. On the beach, the dead man's ashes, Ana said, were sent out to sea on a small, lit boat.

We marveled that as elaborate as the day's events had been, they were no more than a tiny fraction of the ceremonies that attend a death in Bali. On burning day, the central intent is to separate the dead man's soul from his body, and this is accomplished, at bottom, by simply depriving him of a body to be attached to. The elements of his body are resolved and dispersed to *the* elements. Released, he's ready to go. All of which suggests, I'm thinking, the strength of the attachment that must be overcome.

After my mother died, after I had looked into her yellow face a long time, mourning, and the ghouls had come to take her body away to the short fire of the crematorium oven, after that, and after we'd collected the small box of "cremains," my father gathered we three sons together on an Oregon beach for a makeshift ceremony of our own. We waded out at the mouth of the Yachats River into the cold ocean and, with our hands, sifted her remains into the rip side of the waves. So dry. They ran from our fingers outward, toward deeper water. I saw my brother Dale wave his hand back and forth, in a gesture that looked like a blessing, and a wavy white line, bone, appeared on the black sand in front of him. Three faces still lit, and mine must have made four, between gray sky and gray ocean.

(2005)

AT KORÉ'S

::

Izmir, Otel Nil

4 June

Getting lost is usually something I enjoy, the way it calls me to attention. But I had been sufficiently awakened earlier that evening in the closed bazaar, something about how my guide, the creeping Serdar, distrusted every shadow for who might be hiding there. Still, only a couple blocks after setting out alone, I was lost again, the streets empty and poorly lit. I turned, veering away from happiness, wading into the streets. It wouldn't have mattered if I'd turned the other way. At some turns, hell is both ways. I got lost and walked on, not finding my way, that's all. Nothing happened. But a heart will suddenly and inexplicably go into eclipse, and then everything that might have shone like paradise falls, broken, into a netherworld.

Finally, too weary to carry my pride any farther, I flagged a taxi. It whispered insolently through the wet streets, just a few blocks, to the "Otel Nil," my hotel. I paid the cabby and went in. The room was dingy beyond understanding, inducing gloom like only the degradation of green can. Nothing working. Confident roaches. When I went out later for something to drink, prostitutes from Romania were primping at the hall mirror. Just three girls, the not quite extinguished innocence in their faces remembering them as their mothers had known them before they took the bus to Izmir and this. I nodded, I walked by. It was as if, all together, we'd lost some dreadful argument with the gods.

::

She Had Houses

1 June

I'd gone looking for Koré.

My room in Bergama, ancient Pergamum, was charmingly, if decidedly bent. From a bed in the glazed alcove, I stared into an embossed sun on the ceiling, as if there it was never morning, or evening, but always blazing noon. And midday, the sun outside *was* hot; I hoped to avoid it the next morning on my visit to the Temple of Demeter somewhere on the acropolis that leaned over the old town where I was staying.

I made an early start, following a napkin map I'd been given at my pension, out of the twisty streets to where the slopes of the acropolis began; there, I was waylaid by an old Turk in pajamas out walking his Doberman. A decisive fellow. He insisted on saving me the price of admission to the ruins, pointing out with a stick how I could wind my way up the sidehill, not passing go. Game, I set off through the wildflowers, picking a few bright poppies. The hillside itself kept me occupied, for it gave up ancient pottery at every step, and here and there marble bits. Once, twice, I stepped over white columns. So I walked looking at my feet. When I stopped, noticing the rising heat, I saw my guide far below, now looking quite a little man with an insignificant black and brown dog, waving me on left, toward a great shelf. That, apparently, was the way.

Having climbed up, I found Demeter's house was not on top at all, but on the ancient road that snakes down to the lower acropolis. From the time I set foot on the outsize cobble of the way down I saw no one. It was farther than I imagined. Finally, the trail passed above the temple and doubled back down to it. I stopped on the threshold, and then entered. The temple slept in silence on a stone terrace directly over the old city. There were spices everywhere, the air thick with them, and low birdcalls, quiet crickets. I had been up and down all spring, and the ancient myths had begun to speak to me as a way to understand the great swings of my wild heart. And the myth of Demeter and Koré had led me here, to this temple, where myth had once had more than the force of story.

The place is not much visited; the precincts were overgrown. My guidebook, a *Rough Guide* for Turkey, said the "Eleusinian mysteries" had at one time been celebrated at Pergamum, but that characterization had to be loose. The rites at Pergamum had never enjoyed the authority of the mysteries celebrated at Eleusis, though here, too, Demeter and her daughter Koré were remembered, and Hades down under, keeping house in hell. Someone, I saw, had plucked an offering from the aromatic vegetation, had laid it on the temple steps for Demeter and her lost girl. I looked closely, not too wilted; yesterday, probably, someone else had taken the trouble to find this place, to make a gesture with a pilgrim's heart. Leaning over, I looked again, a few herbs, a few flowers, tied with a string.

I reached down to touch the binding twine, deciding then that I would be a pilgrim, too, that when I got back to Athens I would pay my respects to the gods at Eleusis.

::

On the Bus

15 June

There's a public bus from Athens to Elefsina, what was Eleusis when the greater mysteries were celebrated there. The morning man at the Hotel Tembi explained how to catch it, and I was soon on board. Rattles and heat, many unfocused faces, people who would have preferred to be somewhere else, and in their minds, were. I escaped too into my own thinking, rehearsing again the story forever associated with Eleusis, the story of Demeter and her daughter Koré, and Hades who stole the girl away. The story has been told so many times, and every time, perhaps, a little differently. Koré (whose name means girl) goes gathering flowers in a sweet meadow, not with Demeter (whose name means mother), but with friends. Everywhere in the green grasses the girls find flowers, hyacinths and irises, roses and violets; as for Koré, she falls for the narcissus, but when she reaches to take it—tradition insists she reaches for it with both hands—the earth opens under her and out roar the horses of Hades. The god abducts the howling girl to his home in the netherworld. He can do it. Zeus, her father, Hades's brother, has agreed. Demeter, her mother, has not agreed, and when she hears Koré's cries as if from the bottom of a deep well, she sets out to find her lost girl. She asks everyone, but no one dares tell her the terrible news, until Selene, the moon, who knows something, and Helios, the sun, who knows all, find courage enough to speak the truth. Demeter, in a fury, abandons Olympos, abandons the gods.

It's in the guise of an old woman that she appears in Eleusis, there undertaking the care of the son of King Keleos and fair Metaneira. To make the boy immortal, she anoints him with ambrosia and puts him down to sleep among the burning embers on the hearth. However, when Metaneira discovers her child hidden in the fire, she panics, a lapse of confidence that calls forth Demeter's wrath—people, she says, are too stupid to know what's good from what's evil. She shows herself the great goddess, demanding the citizens of Eleusis build her a temple to propitiate her fantastic, and seemingly displaced, anger. They build it on a low hill, what else can they do?

Still, Demeter longs for Koré, and she decides to blackmail the gods to get her back. She visits her wrath on nature: no seed in the earth will be allowed to sprout. When the people starve, they will have nothing to offer to the gods. That way, she reasons, the gods too will finally come to suffer. Unless Zeus relents and calls Koré out of hell, the race of mortals must die out. Zeus gives in, sends fleet Hermes into hell, who convinces Hades to let Koré go. But before she goes, she eats a sweet pomegranate seed when Hades offers it. Carelessly, she eats, under the spell of her joy at the news that she is to be restored above to the shining earth. Hermes sends a whip over the heads of Hades' horses, and with Koré in his cart, drives them out of hell. They emerge into the upper world from the cave at Eleusis.

Koré is reunited with her mother. But with the girl still in her arms, still in their first embrace, Demeter asks Koré the fatal question: did she eat anything down in hell? If she did, she'll have to go back, to spend a third of every year in the netherworld. Koré says *yes*, she did, that Hades *forced her* to eat the red seed (a lie!). Ah, but they are happy, and Demeter restores the earth to resurgent green; life itself is resumed under the sun. Beneficent again, Demeter, the giver of grain, bestows her second gift on the chastened mortals, teaching them how to celebrate her holy rites at Eleusis, revealing the dread mysteries to them. Then, with sweet Koré, she rejoins the gods on Olympos.

I was not so happy; in general, buses do not foster happiness. Still, looking out, there was beauty. The sky was clear, and once we were free of Athens's overbuilt streets, the light loved all things. On the left, the Gulf of Corinth boomed blue, laced with whitecaps, and on it dozens of big ships rode at anchor or found their way to port.

The blacktop here sometimes follows the ancient road between Athens and Eleusis, sometimes not, but, either way, my journey was different in kind from that taken by the initiates on their sacred way to the temple at Eleusis. They had already undergone an initiation into the lesser mysteries, celebrated in spring at Agrai on the banks of the Ilissos, before they undertook the greater mysteries in the fall at Eleusis. And for the mysteries at Eleusis, the initiates, the *mystai*, first prepared in Athens; they were instructed, fasted, underwent ritual bathing, and performed sacrifices. When they set out on the road to Eleusis, then, they were clean. The procession itself, the *pompe*, was a great spectacle. Some walked, some rode in carts. The road was long, fourteen miles; a great train followed the priests and priestesses up front, who themselves followed a wooden statue of the god Iakchos. It was said Iakchos had taken shape out of the cries of the celebrants: the impulse in the cry was known as a god who himself came to lead the way. So, it seems, the *mystai* on the road to Eleusis walked in the wake of their own enthusiasm.

The procession passed the foothills of the Parnes, threaded valleys, stopped at Apollo's sanctuary, at Aphrodite's shrine, passed by the lakes of the Rheitoi to the sea. There, the procession halted, and the *mystai* rested. After sunset, torches were lit and the celebrants marched on, everyone carrying a torch now, a flaming train, into the court at Eleusis.

When the time came, and I arrived in Elefsina, I stepped down quietly enough onto the baked pavement. I do not believe that I can really claim to have arrived at the same place as the *mystai*, though soon enough the distinctive hump of the Eleusinian hill came into view.

If my arrival was mundane, and why not, it was less fraught with dissonance than the 1804 visit of Edward Dodwell, who discovered by the roadside at the edge of the village a statue of Koré standing neck deep in dung. It wasn't disrespect. The local peasantry had remembered the old ways and made an offering of manure to ensure good harvests on the Rarian plain—to renew, really, Demeter's gift of the grain.

::

Her Home Place

Often, traveling, great expectations gnaw the edges of perception. Real seeing emerges only in surprise or retrospect. The Eleusis of the guidebooks, however, doesn't encourage great expectations, doesn't, in fact, encourage a visit. Elefsina is dismissed as an industrial suburb deep in soot. The description served me very well, insulated me from the letdown of "spoiled" places. The Mango Club across the street, The Galaxy built against the wall of the precincts, their low rock music, I had no desire to banish them. I felt Eleusis must sit in my mind with our time; I know from here. Looking at the line of industrial smokestacks behind the sacred hill, I thought of William Carlos Williams's accommodation of industry and the ancients in "Classic Scene," a description of a two-stack powerhouse as a great throne on which two commanding figures, the stacks, sit. The whole line of smokestacks at the cement factory beyond the hill were, in Williams's word, "passive" that day, and seemed to recall, in their shape, a row of outsize classical columns.

My thinking of Williams at Eleusis wasn't altogether a non sequitur. It was Modernism that brought me here, and my initiation to Modernism had itself hinged on the chance purchase of a small volume by Williams, *Kora in Hell*. When, as a graduate student, my interests had turned to Ezra Pound, I had discovered Eleusis at the secret heart of Pound's eccentric eroticism. Indeed, I had gone so far as to write a book on the subject, an attempt to read behind the screen of Pound's *trobar clus* (closed poetry). In the years since then, slowly, I have discovered that the spell of Eleusis, the mysteries, spread very widely in Modernist circles. Some thought they knew what the mystery was; some took the mystery itself as a warrant to write over our unknowing.

To a degree, then, I was on a literary pilgrimage at Eleusis, there to see what the poets I had long studied had only imagined. But more than that I had been drawn to Eleusis by the final mystery of the place, where the secrets were kept, where fear of the divine checked the tongue.

I walked the walled precincts, by prickly pear, wading through blooming yellow, through the pink of oleander, sage, dry grasses the color of wheat, the color of Demeter's hair. I found a fig tree growing against a wall built in the time of Pericles. The fruit was black and soft. I tasted it. I walked on.

::

Another Koré

In the small museum at Eleusis I found again the marble statue of the fleeing girl I had seen in Washington, D.C., some months before. She's a koré, but not Demeter's daughter; usually she's described as one of the "full-breasted daughters" of Okeanos, one of those gathering flowers with Persephone when the earth opened and Hades was there. This statue, I determined, was a copy; the original was still traveling. But it was a good copy, and in it I remembered the original girl. Her lithe running, yes, running beyond concern. Her beautiful, wide face, her veiled eyes, terrifyingly composed. Again I noticed how from the side this koré's lips are cruel—she saves herself without compunction, but looks back, across her body, wanting to see just how it goes with her friend. Finally, however, even her curiosity is limited. It's as if in running she knows, more than anything, herself running.

::

Thinking It Over

The hill at Eleusis is low and I walked up a ways, taking a seat in a stony place, with the *telesterion* in prospect. It is there, in the *telesterion*, that the mysteries were celebrated for some two thousand years. The initiates were pledged to silence, and they held to their pledge. There is no credible report of what went on in the *telesterion* on mystery night from all the teeming crowds, the centuries of crowds, who crossed the threshold there, who emerged, it is said, less burdened by the fear of death, of hell. Closing my eyes, I struggled to really get my mind, my heart, around this, to fully credit the sheer size of this silence. The divine here must have been felt as a force far more palpable than the lips of a lover or a hard man's fist. There are laws forbidding murder and incest, but those laws are broken, aren't real enough to stay the finger on the trigger or a hand straying across a daughter's breast. I could not imagine it, finally, how a culture, and the divine within a culture, could have spoken with such authority for so long. I wasn't even sure I could like it: I must be of my time and my place and that means both distant and less constrained.

Still, I sensed a presence welling out of the *telesterion*, which must have shone as a great light on mystery night. If I can't judge its depth or extent, I know it must have been brighter and bigger than whatever I can know.

There is a long history of speculation about what went on down there. They were making guesses in Christ's time. Ezra Pound thought that a *hierogamia,* a sacred union, was celebrated by hierophants at Eleusis. For him, the mysteries failed when the sacred sex was no longer performed by priests and priestesses, when they brought "whores for Eleusis" to do the job. But I can't countenance the contempt in that word "whores." I remember again the innocence in the eyes of the prostitutes in Izmir, remember the compassion Pound so often forgot. Prostitutes, after all, were not forbidden the mysteries at Eleusis.

Others imagined a marriage was performed in the *telesterion*, perhaps celebrated with *phallos* and *cteis;* still others thought the *mystai* must have been given drugs (ergot or opium), or that, after a staging of the story of Koré and Demeter, an ear of wheat was revealed, that the cycle of the wheat told through the myth itself heartened the initiates, through death a rebirth into blessedness. Some argued for a birth, either a child to Koré or Koré reborn from her deathly sojourn with Hades, emerging again from earth like new shoots from the death of the buried kernels of wheat.

Of course, the theorists, every one, have felt constrained to discredit the rest of their kind. It's amusing to watch them, and in the name of truth, try to exert a sovereignty over this place, a white ruin, where the stones do not speak.

My reading about Eleusis has been desultory enough. The book that made the strongest impression on me is George Mylonas' *Eleusis and the Eleusinian Mysteries*. I confess, however, that it is not his scholarship or argumentation that moves me; it is Mylonas' own story. He worked for years on a dig at Eleusis, fired by the great ambition to unveil the mysteries. The archaeologists dug and dug, expecting to find in the dirt some key, perhaps a secret compartment from which the god in the machine could have been made to appear. They didn't find it. *They dug the site to bedrock.* Slowly, Mylonas moved from the side of the theorists to siding against them, arguing again and again against their speculations. He seems to have finally found peace in not knowing, in accepting that the mysteries would remain mysteries. It's this movement of his heart, his affirmation of unknowing, that speaks to me now.

I am not alone in this. Even the popular literature available at the site, even the guidebooks, take refuge in our not knowing. Perhaps the straggling tourists at Eleusis have not earned it with a shovel or long hours in a library, but something in final ignorance appeals to them. It is the story we hear at Eleusis in our time, and brimming, I think, with its own mythological content. But, for it to matter, you must lean into that not knowing, suffer it, lean far enough to feel in your unknowing that you, also, are one of those you cannot know.

::

Ploutonion

I got around to the cave last, as if my walking had been a long, preparatory, spiraling in. Except for Koré and Demeter and Hades down under, the *plutonion* is a cave like any other. But all caves, even shallow ones, share in a common mysteriousness, as if the earth might speak here, from this mouth. There's a slit in the back of the cave, and darkness behind that. This is an entrance to hell; there are many in Greece and not only Greece. But in Koré and Demeter's story, it's also an exit *from* hell, which is rarer, much rarer. We are all of us going, but few make the return. Even having the entrance localized is reassuring; hell seems most times somehow more ubiquitous, a potentiality in every moment, in every place.

Standing right where Koré emerged after two years with Hades in the underworld, I dreamed of her again. She was only a girl when she was carried off down under. Returning, it was springtime; it must have seemed that she had stepped into the griddle of the sun, hot and dazzling as only long seclusion can make the sun. In the Homeric Hymn, she's carried up in a cart behind horses, but I see her climbing out, slender and pale-limbed, still girlish, but not a girl. Perhaps the insects have begun to buzz and that buzzing must seem intolerably loud to the dazzled Koré, who barely recognizes her mother, Demeter, in the light swarming around her. But she knows her. They embrace, and for a minute, it's as if the air were resolved into bird song, as if Koré were a girl again. And then the mother asks the freighted question, a question that must be answered with a *yes*, because life on earth can never be allowed to become a paradise. "Oh, Koré, did you eat anything while you were underground?" Oh Koré, you are still so innocent for all that you have suffered! "Yes, mother," she says, "I was hungry, I ate a few pomegranate seeds, just a few seeds." It is enough. That paradise of happiness, the promise of forever that a moment before had seemed real in the embrace of mother and daughter, is checked. "Koré, Koré, then you will have to go back, have to spend a third of every year with Hades in the netherworld!" Standing there, in the cave at Eleusis, I wondered about those seeds, the finality of it all. Neither Koré nor Demeter rebel. There was a pact with Zeus: eat and return to hell. They accept, and Koré gets used to the sun, finds it more like home than not, resolves to live in it her months on earth. She begins to see flowers, a flowering meadow, which appears again only under her gaze.

Somehow, in eating the seeds she acquiesced to hell, to Hades. Having done so, she entered into the great polarity, of hell and sweet earth, of depression and earthly joy.

Standing there, I thought of Hades, who lost his girl. She has returned above, to the world beautiful and full of tangles. I imagine him scaling the dark rocks after her, up narrow chimneys, through wet places and dry, until he sees the narrow opening and the sun raging, it seems to him, all fire. Koré and Demeter have already gone away. Eight months. He waits until the sun has set and the moon risen, a late moon; the white slipper of Selene presses on his heart. Almost unknowing, he slips out into the moonlight and the starlight, for the stars are everywhere, strange to him and too bright. Their beauty hurts him, but he submits; forever now he will be a man scarred by shining stars.

I emerged slowly from my dreaming. On a sandy shelf in the very mouth of hell there were several little offerings, wildflowers and herbs plucked from the precincts. Without a common culture, it's hard to know what the mind was thinking when the hand made the offering—to honor or to placate or just to witness that this is sacred ground. I was surprised to discover in my own heart an offering, too. Casting about I saw what looked to be a fig tree growing down out of the ceiling of the cave. It must have been cut to a nub between last year and this but had responded by sending out several shoots sideways, each two or three feet long, in leaf, angling for more light. On my tiptoes I was able to pluck a leaf, which I set on the sand with the other gifts.

(2001)

OF *CORSE*

::

1.

Hommage à W. G. Sebald

My father, an old man now, volunteered for service in World War II. He didn't have to; born in 1912, he was already old enough when the U.S. entered the war that he would not have been drafted. He chose the Navy, and although he'd never been to sea, he was given command of his own slow ship, the *S.S. George Flavel*. When he told us boys about his years at sea, he never let us imagine that there had been anything grand about it. The *George Flavel* was a Liberty ship configured as a troop carrier. If not literally built in a day, it had been hastily constructed in the shipyards of Portland, Oregon. My father made the actual sailing sound uneventful. If once or twice in a convoy or alone on the Pacific they had a fright, the dreaded submarines and the Japanese Zeros never showed up. To hear him talk about it, the *George Flavel* shuttled lightly over the waves between Seattle and Hawaii and Alaska, occasionally running on out to Guam.

Though the blood had only been dry for four years when I was born, it seemed to me, a very small boy, that the war had happened ages before, that my father's war had been undertaken in a world very different than the one outside our door. What most entranced me in my father's stories were his descriptions of the tricks of light played on sailors in the far north, on the Bering Sea and in the straits between Alaska and the Soviet Union. He said sometimes fishing villages appeared on the horizon from a great distance out. Most, he said, were in Alaska, but on occasion they saw tiny towns in Siberia as well (that sounded far away indeed). The odd thing, my father said, was that although those villages were beyond the horizon, the arctic air raised them up on tall, black cliffs, hung them in the sky over what should have been open sea. How I loved to imagine those small villages built on vertiginous heights at the sea's edge, the houses glowing with unearthly light.

I believed my father's stories implicitly, but I think he had proof as well, small photographs taken with a box Brownie tucked under black corners in an album of photos from that time, my father a dashing man in dress blues and a white, officer's hat, my mother a wraith in a long, wool coat.

I heard about the great cliffs reared up as if by magic a lifetime ago. Nevertheless, I remember clearly, as the most telling detail in my father's story, that if they steamed toward one of the sky villages, the cliffs came down, until, if they put into port, the little town that had appeared on high had slipped right down to the water's edge, and, my father said quietly, you could disembark and step right into its muddy streets. And he had, he said. He'd walked through what had been mirage, a magical village.

::

I was thinking of my father as I climbed the great ramps from the water up to *la ville haute* at Bonifacio—because here the mirage is not dissipated by the sailor's arrival, here the city remains improbably suspended sky high on chalky cliffs. At the southern tip of Corsica, the upper city of Bonifacio looks across a narrow strait to Sardinia. The drop is sheer on all sides, more than sheer on some, the limestone cliffs having calved away to present the town on a tee. The situation looks so unlikely that approaching the great gate you wouldn't be surprised to meet a smiling magician, perched on a rock, his hand elegantly gesturing toward his finest apparition.

At the top of the final incline (*la montée Saint-Roch*), I crossed the heavy planks that have replaced the drawbridge, drawn up often in more dangerous centuries. Now it's a stroll through the fortified gate into the old town. Most of the buildings that crowd the thumb-shaped promontory date from the occupation by Genoa: hundreds of years of standing here, most of them three to five floors over the narrow alleys that wind through their mud-colored walls. Like my father's fishing villages in the far north, *la ville haute* is real enough, though sufficient magic clings to it that travelers arrive from around the world just to walk here. In season, I've heard, they crowd the alleys liked schooled fish, rubbing against one another to get through. But I walked unencumbered at the end of May, eyes on the brown buildings, noticing how the walls flare out near the street to bear the immense weight of the limestone. Many of the larger buildings have stone buttresses, and flying buttresses cross the alleys overhead, here and there, to discourage leaning.

If you're not looking out from the upper city, peering over the ramparts, you wouldn't know you were so high up, walking in the sky of those down around the harbor or out at sea. No, in *la ville haute* you walk as if at the bottom of stony defiles. You feel low down rather than high up. The years have sifted deeply into these alleys, these old buildings, and in their age they have achieved an almost impenetrable stillness. You feel the way they have settled into time and endured. Walking these alleys, you wade through the years. The old buildings speak low in a guttural growl, like a big dog that means it. It is necessary to walk quietly to draw close, to avoid sudden movements.

Around the few tiny squares and the wider, if still narrow alleys, a ribbon of bright tourist shops masks the massive gravity of the place. I reminded myself, walking by, that such shops everywhere reflect the desires of their clientele. Although travelers are called here by the suspended city, they crowd around the only bright things in sight, the taut awnings and racks of shiny postcards, the varieties of kitsch, the rushing waiters carrying out plates of food to be set down on loud tablecloths. Small shops selling *charcuterie* or olive oil, or case knives and switchblades, most bearing the brand name *vendetta*. It's here the tourists spend most of their time and are most at ease, their faces alive, talking, hands gesturing. I think they cluster around the new, bright shops and restaurants to avoid the judgment of the old buildings, buildings that insist we cannot stay.

When I turned from the old, brown houses to the tourists and the world they have called up here in *la ville haute*, the travelers seemed to flicker, insubstantial, like characters in a movie projected on a rippling sheet. But perhaps I am again thinking of my father, who has reached that age when everyone, or almost everyone, he knew as a boy is dead and visible—if at all—only in the grainy frames of his memory. Wandering the alleys, my own person felt pale enough. I glanced into open doors, saw the stairs up, some as steep as ladders. Everything was smaller inside than I would have imagined, the thickness of the walls diminishing the enclosed volumes. The shops tiny, restaurants crowded in under low ceilings, tables pushed up against rough, unplastered stone. As if time, perhaps, had pressed the walls in, pulled the ceilings down. I wasn't quite sure I liked the feel of the interior spaces, or maybe it felt like the little rooms weren't welcoming to the likes of me, a shambling guy, bigger I imagine than the folks who built these places. When it started to rain, the streets cleared, and I walked around under the visor of my cap for a good while, the buildings more present than before, wet and glistening. Red sand in rough stucco. Soon I'd been down every alley, but that doesn't mean I'd actually seen them. Seeing takes a lot of looking.

The real bustle in Bonifacio is not in the upper city at all, but concentrated in a narrow strip around the snug harbor, inside *le goulet*. Yachts crowd the docks, and cruise ships and ferries are regularly in evidence. Even in late May the sidewalks were thick with strollers, and a solid wall of outside seating for restaurants dominated the quay. Money breeds near water, apparently, like mosquitoes. But back when the buildings in *la ville haute* were getting built, the money was there, on high, hoarded by a few families. Fishermen and sailors were not welcome and made their lives by water. They had a church of their own in the lower town, built in the thirteenth century and dedicated to the patron saint of sailors, Érasme. It's still there, though hard to see walking by, because the neighboring buildings look to have grown over it. If it ever had a significant exterior it hasn't got one now. Inside, however, the crowding doesn't show. The church is small but whole. I sat in a pew and let the smell of seawater and incense wash around me. I thought of my father and stood again to light a candle, not believing, but taking a moment to turn toward him. We're caught together in a rip tide.

I let my gaze wander. The few little pews awkward on a checked floor. I leaned back and noticed overhead, unexpected, that a small schooner had been hung from the ceiling over the congregation, a primitive model of a four master. It caught a little light up there, what must have been reflected light, and shone quietly against the dark, unfinished wood that lined the church's simple vault. Afloat on prayers for safe harbor, I suppose, but oddly sinking the congregation beneath the imagined waves, "full fathom five" under the four master's brown keel. Sitting there, I remembered loving the quicksilver sheen of water's surface seen from the bottom side, swimming underwater in sea or lake. But from down there everything that floated, buoyant, had looked broken at the waterline. It had all felt faintly disturbing. The little schooner, I noticed, had no sheets to the wind, but floated soberly overhead; it seemed to have found sanctuary. But looking closely, I could see that even here, under Saint-Érasme's care, three tiny blue lifeboats hung over the side, at the ready. My reverie was interrupted by the arrival of a French tour group. Whisked in, they listened to an explanation, then trooped right back out again. A few stayed behind for a moment to cross themselves or pray or, like me, to light a candle, stealing a moment of sanctuary, too. But I was surprised that not one of them looked up at the little schooner suspended overhead.

Outside, walking again up the great ramps to *la ville haute*, I remembered that when I was a boy my father had strung a big balsa wood jet in the sky over my bed, on transparent fishing line, and how waiting for sleep, I'd felt like I was outside, stretched out on the lawn, plane spotting. The blue jet with its red star insignias had been handmade by my uncle Cecil, after his return from the Korean War. I can't quite remember my father putting it up; it was there already as far back as memory goes, an invitation to imagined flight.

Again I passed through the narrow canyons of the upper city, the sleeping buildings, and out of the citadel onto the open ground of the promontory. I looked over the ramparts down at the harbor often claimed to be the stronghold Lamus in Book Ten of Homer's *Odyssey*, home to the Laestrygonians. It hadn't proven a safe harbor for Odysseus' sailors; in Homer's account, they died here. By sword and knife and rocks flung from the headlands. Their boats scuttled, those Greeks were speared "like fish" in the water. Only Odysseus, who had thought to tie up his "blue-prowed" boat outside the jaws of the harbor, was able to escape, exhorting his shipmates, in Robert Fagles's translation, to,

> "Put your backs in the oars—now row or die!"
> In terror of death they ripped the swells—all as one—
> And what a joy as we darted out to open sea,
> Clear of those beetling cliffs . . . my ship alone.

Whether or not the identification of the Homeric Lamus with Bonifacio is correct, the situation is clearly favored, and people have lived here for a long time. Even the Genoese constructions in the upper city could be considered recent. Indeed, if Bonifacio is Homer's Lamus, the place would have already been ancient when Odysseus and his companions rowed in. The oldest human remains found on Corsica were discovered here, in a sea cave at *l'Araguina*. Called *La Dame de Bonifacio*, she walked this ground and died here about 6570 B.C. And *La Dame de Bonifacio* wasn't found where she dropped. She'd been buried. There had been a ceremony, her remains sprinkled with yellow ochre. You can see her bones at the *Museé de l'Alta Rocca*.

::

I stepped back from the ramparts overlooking *le goulet* and kept walking, out toward the end of the headlands. I'd recently been thinking about the archaic, about the status we confer on things pre-historical. Age doesn't always confer authority, or perhaps the authority of age can easily be undercut by words, by recorded history. Words want to crowd in. Archaic things seem better able to resist language, to render flimsy the guesses of archaeologists, professional and amateur alike. So the things themselves push forward, authoritative and mute. We feel age in them, a rude presence. Dry and austere.

Rather belatedly, it seemed to me, I realized that the Bonifician promontory itself is shaped like a ship's hull, and indeed the locals must have noticed this fact long ago, because the up-jutting rock in the sea just off land's end is called *le gouvernail*, the rudder, a conceit which would put the *L'église de Saint-Érasme* very near the prow on the land side.

I was heading for *le cimetière marin*, a cluster of small crypts within whitewashed walls. Not so old. Neat, and most of these dead are not forgotten, to judge by the candles burning in many of the vaults. *"Ici Repose,"* the inscriptions begin, almost all of them.

Tiled roofs over simple vaults. Whole families. Fathers and sons, mothers and daughters, *ici,* here. I read the names and glanced up just in time to see a couple in red pants stroll through, looking like lost golfers, through the crypts that taken together suggest a tiny town, a model town. Somehow *le cimetière marin* hardly suggests mortality, with its clean lines and windswept walks. The polished stone of the family vaults and freshly whitewashed monuments thus far seem to have largely resisted time. This, oddly enough, feels unsatisfactory, and I found myself returning in my walking again and again to the one blighted tomb, where the effects of weather seem to have been mysteriously concentrated. On inspection, I realized that the ruined state of the tomb had more to do with the low quality of the construction than with anything else. A small, classical shrine, it had been built from terracotta, from bricks and tiles. All the fine detail, the four fluted columns and the prominent entablature and pediment, even the diminutive dome, ribbed with rounded terracotta tiles, had been worked out of impermanent plaster and just painted over. At one time the whole structure might have been yellow. In any case, the paint has mostly washed away and a good deal of the plaster lies in rubble around the foot of the shrine. Strangely, even the rude iron cross that stands in front of the little building has been half eaten away by Bonifacio's salty winds. The interior of the shrine itself has apparently long been exposed to the weather: one of a pair of narrow doors is stuck open. I surprised myself by squeezing inside. A small statue of Mary in what was once a blue niche presides over a gaudy, painted altar, where two crosses and a pair of bleached wooden candlesticks stand crookedly on top of a bit of wind-blown lace. The floor is littered with debris. Back outside, I noticed an inscription over the door, *virginis immaculatae conceptae*. The crypt is in the ground, under, hacked out of the limestone of the plateau; the way down is too narrow, the ceiling too low, for me to descend, but I peered into the shadows. There are still berths available, roughhewn into the raw walls.

::

That evening, I ate dinner on a small terrace under an olive tree, across the street and up a hillside from the *Hôtel des Étrangers*. Black bread, apples, a few olives, a little wine. I was reading again W.G. Sebald's *Campo Santo*, a posthumously published miscellany that includes a few pieces of a book on Corsica he left unfinished at the time of his death in 2002. The reading itself felt clairvoyant. Maybe it was, maybe reading should be. The small shadows of the olive leaves shifted in the puddled light on the tabletop, like fish. I read the title essay slowly, winding my way through the eighteen pages of its single, luminous paragraph. *Campo santo*, holy ground, refers to a graveyard, specifically in Sebald's essay to a neglected graveyard near Piana that he investigated one hot afternoon. As readers of Sebald's work know, the particulars of experience often undergo startling expansions in his prose, in the lucid associations of his mind. Sebald levitates out of the little graveyard in Piana, where he had stooped to examine the wild grasses, and, leaping from association to association, he soon has transported us from specifically Corsican funerary practices and folkways to a meditation on the diminishing place of the dead in our lives, how life without memory, forgetting, has usurped almost everything. Any act of remembrance, in Sebald's telling, is a tack into the wind.

I closed the book. On the island, in French, the name for Corsica is *Corse*, which oddly enough in English is a variant spelling of corpse. I remembered this not at once but in time; it rattled out of my brain where it had lodged a long time ago, when I was a student of Middle English literature, where the usage is common. Etymologically, the root of both words has for centuries wound around the idea of the body. The body unencumbered by living. Perhaps my mood had darkened with the coming evening. But then, in what felt like an illuminated rhyme of Sebald's *campo santo*, the word *corpusant* swam into consciousness, *corpo santo*, holy body. Out of Melville, I imagine, *Moby Dick*. The more common name for Melville's "corpusants" is St. Elmo's Fire, that unearthly glow that sometimes, in extreme weather, made of the masts flaming candles on old sailing ships. And, to close the circle, St. Elmo is another name for Saint-Érasme, whose church I had lingered in earlier in the day, just a few hundred yards away, in Bonifacio.

::

2.

Hommage à Dorothy Carrington

Reading Sebald, it was clear he'd been reading Dorothy Carrington, her *Dream-Hunters of Corsica*. I recognized the influence right away. He doesn't try to hide it, either, citing her in the body of his text. It had been Carrington, rather than Sebald, who had first called my attention to the island, convinced me I wanted to make a visit, and although Carrington's characterizations of the Corsican *mazzeri* had worked their way into my imagination, as they had Sebald's, I knew from having read her *Corsica: Portrait of a Granite Island*, that the dream-hunters interested her first and foremost as yet another manifestation of the archaic in Corsican life, not in a distant past, but in the Corsica just going.

The *mazzeri*, I'd never run across anything quite like them in a lifetime of reading. At night, the *mazzeri* go hunting, out into the maquis, and they kill the first animal they meet, maybe a pig or a goat or a cow, but perhaps even a wild boar. Some, mostly men, shoot their prey, but the women do their killing with a stick or a cudgel or, hunting in packs, "with their teeth, like hounds." As her informant explained it to Carrington, "When they've killed the animal they roll it on its back, and then they recognize in its face someone belonging to their village. The next morning they tell what they have done, and the person they name always dies within a year."

Carrington reports several conflicting accounts concerning the status of the hunting; some insisted the *mazzeri* never left their beds, hunted in their dreams alone, while others thought the *mazzeri* were physically abroad at night, hunting in a trance or sleepwalking, while still others believed the *mazzeri* left a body in their bed *and* hunted in the maquis. In any case, it was agreed they could be heard hunting at night, calling out in human voices or baying like dogs. If Carrington's stories about the dream-hunters sound frankly incredible, she is herself a credible witness, and her reports are by no means unique; there is a considerable literature surrounding the practices of the *mazzeri*, and their powers were widely acknowledged in the villages where they lived—their reports were accepted as true. Although the news they brought must have often been unwelcome, the dream-hunters were not seen as personally responsible for their behavior or for the deaths they foresaw. It was understood that they were, "called—as the Corsicans say—by an imperious unseen power."

::

The Air Corsica flight I had boarded in Nice landed at Figari-Sud, at Figari, a village of less than seven hundred between Bonifacio and Porto-Vecchio. Carrington reports that in living memory there were a dozen *mazzeri* active in Figari, three as recently as 1975. The image of my silver jet dropping out of the sky into a world that had accommodated the dream-hunters just yesterday, that's the kind of thing that can make Corsica feel uncanny, the contemporary and the archaic pressed side by side. It was the proximity of the archaic that drew Carrington to Corsica in the first place, at least it was the archaic in Corsican life to which she most responded. The word is everywhere in her work, her Corsica. By the time she wrote *The Dream-Hunters*, she had come to see the *mazzeri* as the most archaic of all Corsican traditions, as antedating even the megalithic menhirs that first entranced her. She argues in *The Dream-Hunters* that the nocturnal world of the *mazzeri* derives directly from Corsica's pre-agrarian past, a world contemporary with *La Dame de Bonifacio*, but not altogether extinguished even now. To the skeptical presumptions of modern archaeology, I imagine her careful arguments are not proof, but her Corsica speaks, and not only to me. She remains the best known of all of Corsica's apologists. What is most compelling about Carrington's Corsica, perhaps, is that the traces of the archaic she describes aren't on some distant, animist island in the Indonesian archipelago, but so much nearer home, very near the heart of Europe—a few miles south of France, a few miles west of Italy—which calls the archaic close for us westerners, and, perhaps, calls to the archaic in us.

::

And so I found myself driving up a curvy road to Sartène, described incessantly, in Prosper Mérimée's phrase, as "the most Corsican of Corsican towns." Mérimée visited in 1839; that his characterization has stuck says something about the place and something about the persistence of a well-turned phrase. It suggests a place traditional, but the word *town* probably qualifies that, over against villages, many of which must be more traditional than Sartène. Still, the town does feel like it's looking back rather than forward, and that's fine by me. The modern is ever more homogenous, and homogeneity leeches out the reason from travel. I was staying for over a week in Sartène and that seemed like a long time to the hotel staff, but it was a visit, no more. Dorothy Carrington came to Corsica in 1948 and stayed, pretty much continuously, until she died. Over fifty years. She published *Corsica: Portrait of a Granite Island* in 1971, *The Dream-Hunters* in 1995. She wrote books steeped in the years, the kind of books you can write only if you write about only one place. Admirable. And yet, this is not the common way of knowing, not how we travel, and though I admire her books I don't aspire to one place. I have restless feet, a malady, perhaps, but one I share with most travelers, even serious travelers.

::

I ventured out into the town walking, ground truthing in the earth scientists' fine phrase, seeing if what I'd read would be what I found. The buildings were there, great blocks of dressed granite, almost all of them. Gray and it was raining, so very gray, dour in the extreme. The buildings were almost colorless, as if the whole place had been shot in black and white, and my umbrella put a black sky over everything. Still, there were the trees and flowers, their colors vivified by the contrast. Here, too, a world narrow and twisty, streets and little alleys, none of them straight, walled in by the granite buildings. Everything weathered and up and down. In Bonifacio, all the climbing is on the ramps between the town on the water and the town on the promontory, which themselves are more or less on the level. But Sartène hangs on a hillside, and although the streets running parallel to it slope only a little, anything up or down is steep, stepped, and often enough a dead fall. It's an excellent town for suicidal jumps but dangerous for stumblers. A knee-high stone wall is often all there is to keep you from a thirty-foot drop into a stony thicket. The pavers in the alleys are granite, also, as are the stairs. A little asphalt has been spread on a few of the main streets but not on many. A few of the walls have been stuccoed and painted but in most cases so long ago that the paint is suggested by no more than a hint of color; the gray undertones dominate. In the rain and fog, the Golfe du Valinco stirs in its bed out of seeing, far down the Rizzanese valley. Still, I know it's there, another world on a sunny day, peacock blue in the distance.

In Sartène, in rain or sun, you soon come round to the *Place de la Libération*, the small heart of the town. You can enter or leave *La Place* from eight different directions, and they're all interesting, or you can stay, sit in one of the cafés for hours. I chose the café *La Victoire*, a small round table with a jade-green top, very old, deep under the awning. The rain let up. Children chasing a soccer ball on *La Place*. An Irish setter puppy tussling with a hound with a bandaged foot. As if materializing out of the air, a few old fellows stood around a gray-bearded man in a black fedora, looking conspiratorial. Late afternoon. Quick espressos or a glass of wine. Friends at tables. Families. Tables of men eyeing the ladies. Always someone coming, someone going.

Evening. I paid my tab and walked across *La Place* and into the Church of St. Mary, wondering if it was here that a priest had performed an exorcism on a *mazzeru*, a man who wanted to be freed from his dreaming, as reported by Dorothy Carrington. Inside, I inspected the enormous cross and chain used in the *Procession du Cantenacciu* every year on Good Friday, when a penitent dons a pointed red cowl and red robe and carries the cross and drags the chain through the night streets of Sartène, his identity hidden, pelted by a howling crowd. To get clean.

Back outside, I turned around the corner of the church and started down an alley, *Rue du Purgatoire*, as it turned out. All things considered, it's surprisingly narrow. A patch of granite on a rough wall had recently been plastered over, smooth and white, perfect for graffiti. As if in homage to Dorothy Carrington, the wall had been tagged with blue and red handprints. Very like the handprints that figure so prominently in many of the most archaic human sites in the world. The archaic impulse still alive in us now. I looked at my hands, humming in the low light of the alley. So central to desire, it's with hands that we reach for.

Less encouraging, I thought, the graffiti included the botched English plural *book's* and, set off by itself in a cartouche, the single French word *mal*.

I walked on, wondering how the tagger had meant that, and did the *mal* refer to the books or to the handprints or to a sickened feeling about life? Or had the word been turned on me, reading it, had it been printed there as an act of malevolence? As I walked on down the alley, I noticed that there were no opportunities to turn right, not once before you reached the dead end, but that there were many opportunities to turn left, to the sinister side, and I wondered if this might be related to how the alley got its name. I walked the alley clear to the end. Coming back, of course, all the turnings were right, narrow stairs built of granite blocks down into *la vielle ville*. But it's all old, really, and austere, a beauty not welcoming but implacable. Beautifully pieced stone walls, life stark in the alleys, men shifting this way and that just to pass one another. It occurred to me that single-file alleys like these bring individuals forward, pick them out from their fellows. You see people either up against a wall or striding along the edge of a dead drop, and there is something about a man silhouetted against a fall that calls up the precariousness of living, the deep valley adrift in shredded clouds for a backdrop.

::

Dorothy Carrington first came to Corsica at the invitation of Jean Cesari, who was working at the time as a waiter in a London dive. He promised Carrington archaic stone statues, "lying forgotten under the olive trees." And he delivered. Carrington herself was there when many of the menhirs at Filitosa were discovered; she saw a great stone that had been lying face down for millennia turned over to greet the sun. She was there when an unsuspected cache of the menhirs, cannibalized into a wall built later by the Toreens, was first uncovered. She helped call attention to the finds, to remember the stones that had been forgotten. Carrington responded powerfully to the menhirs, aesthetically, and because they suggested that the archaic might be right there on the surface of things and yet go unremarked. In the years to come, she found souvenirs of the archaic in Corsica almost everywhere she looked.

I wanted to see the menhirs, too. So I drove out to Filitosa (not far from Sartène). It was raining when I walked, curious, down through the olive trees under the black arc of my umbrella. I envied Carrington then, when I heard the sound of pan flutes rising up out of the Bose speaker system that now runs throughout the extensive grounds. I envied her again when I walked within range of the canned commentary at the first standing stone, crackling from a separate speaker system, attached to a standard with four color-coded buttons, each for a different language.

The button-pusher was a German girl who was not listening very closely. She was plugged into her own sounds, fiddling with an MP3 player hanging around her neck. And yet, for all the packaging, the stone statue exerted itself. Not as it had for Carrington, no doubt, just rolled into the sun—it was the very one—but still, forcefully. Although the menhirs at Filitosa are celebrated for the seeming individuality of their faces, the faces struck me as quite abstract. Here a wavy line indicates the swoop of the jaw and there a raised lump a droopy nose, and no more. And the body just a great rectilinear block of stone. The sword and the dagger, however, are realism itself. Which is not to say the faces aren't powerful, but the work is finer on the weapons.

I waded through the deep, wet grass that covered much of the site, the panpipes following me everywhere. I was thinking about Carrington's descriptions of the houses of Corsican country people, as she first saw them, undecorated except for a few beautiful guns hanging on the walls. That pride of place rhymed, I thought, with the careful depictions of the great sword and dagger on the menhir. Even if the weaponry signified rank, suggested a chieftain, perhaps, the fact that the sign was a sword rather than a ring or a brooch insisted on their role in constituting status, perhaps even identity. This was a very Carrington thought, I realized, the way I was pulling the archaic closer.

But we cede authority to the archaic without even thinking about why. First things first. For awhile, things just get old, are used; then they start to appreciate as antiques; by the time you get back to Ancient Greece or Egypt, any bit of it is significant. Further back, the cave art of Lascaux or Altamira for instance, speaks with unchallenged authority. Things that were of little or no value when they were dropped to the ground, a broken bone awl, say, by a contemporary of *La Dame de Bonifacio*, left for trash, might now turn up in a little museum somewhere. We get superstitious, perhaps, but it's undeniable that great age confers its own authority on human artifacts.

Recently, I felt the power of the archaic in a quite absurd way. I read in the papers that a new study of bits of human DNA discovered in coprolites found in my home state, in Oregon, had conclusively set back the date of the human occupation of the Americas to over fourteen thousand years, a thousand years before the long, stubbornly held belief that the makers of Clovis spear points and arrowheads had arrived first. It's ridiculous, I know, but that fossilized shit made me proud of my Oregon roots. "We," somehow, had been first. At least until an older first is discovered.

::

I settled into Sartène, walking for hours and sitting once or twice a day at my jade-green table at *La Victoire*. I listened to a concert there, traditional music sung in Corsican. I watched the bustle of a Saturday market. Jean Henri, the waiter most about at *La Victoire*, treated me like a regular, occasionally bringing me an espresso on the house, "*un cadeau*." Tourists on motorcycles peeled off their leathers and sat in the sun or under the awnings of *La Victoire* or one of the other cafés. I began to recognize the denizens of the place, the real regulars, who had their favorite tables, just like me. The granite buildings rose up in my imagination, until I knew it was a world I could dream in, that even asleep I would know my turnings. I began to wonder about Dorothy Carrington's fifty years in Corsica, if she, approaching a death in her nineties, at an age when death could no longer come as a surprise, if she imagined some night a dream-hunter might strike a boar with a stick, turn it over to discover something of her face in the face of the animal? I don't believe the thought would have disturbed her.

She died in 2002 and was buried in the *cimetière marin* in Ajaccio, just up the coast, her home for decades. By an unlikely chance, this was only a few weeks after W.G. Sebald had died in an auto accident in Norfolk, near his home in East Anglia. So they have left this place, this Corsica, to a modernity that neither of them much fancied, and to encroaching forgetfulness.

::

Some days I drove out of town, into the Sartenais, on roads often too narrow for two cars to pass, out through the satiny-green maquis. I visited the megalithic sites on the Caurian plateau, the *Alignement de Paddaghiu* and the *Alignement de Stantari*, aware that after Filitosa even menhirs without faces had the force of people for me, looming presences.

The great alignments stand like a crowd of the dead gathered together for a long time. Many of them, of course, have been set back up by archaeologists, having toppled sometime in the deep centuries. Many more lie only an edge out of the dirt or not showing at all, left buried, not exhumed. And yet the green is on, here near the end of May. A world rededicated to living. The maquis shines, even some of the menhirs are bright with lichen blooms. Here in the Sartenais.

::

3.

Hommage à Prosper Mérimée

I was surprised at *Stantari* to read on the placard, at the very top, that Prosper Mérimée had visited the site in 1839, on his own tour of Corsica. He got to the site well ahead of the archaeologists, and I'm not sure what there would have been for him to see, a great gathering of menhirs all fallen down. The site is isolated, and it would have been a long ride on a horse to get there in 1839. The pull of the archaic must have been strong in him as well. Mérimée, remembered best as the author of *Carmen,* had been drawn to Corsica by its fearsome reputation, a place backward at the heart of Europe, famous for its vendettas. I'd read his Corsican tale, *Colomba,* in a darkened cabin high over the Atlantic, on the flight over. I'd expected something fusty, a period piece, I don't know why. But *Colomba* feels modern, the power of the old ways of vendetta stand up starkly against the more continental consciousness of Orso della Rebbia, returning at last to his Corsican homeland, only to be met by his sister, Colomba, who prevails on him to do his duty, to avenge his father, all against his will. And he is forced to. The red heart that drives vendetta is revealed, implacable, terrible, yes, but also terribly compelling.

Mérimée modeled his story loosely on a contemporary vendetta in a village nearby Sartène, Fozzano. He met the real Colomba (née Carabelli) at the time of his visit—not the young beauty portrayed in the book—but carrying in her raw the spirit of vendetta. Mérimée took from her what his story needed, in that act of bloodless vampirism so tightly bound up with the art of writing. Of course, I drove the serpentine road over to Fozzano. I had to. The village had the look of a miniature Sartène, a beautiful place if austere. Here, too, the ground breaks away sharply throughout the town, making for many a good place to stumble into a dramatic fall. Flowers grew wildly against the rough granite walls, splashy geraniums planted right in the ground. Here and there a tiny terraced garden, a few vegetables picked out by stone and worked earth. Here and there a fig with its leaves splayed out like a hand. The place didn't seem large enough to have taken sides in a vendetta. But the village had been split between opposing factions for nearly a hundred years before the insult that sparked the fight that incited the bloody vendetta that Colomba figured in. But all vendettas are bloody, and in the nineteenth century an active vendetta in a Corsican village was the rule, not the exception. The Sartenais was notorious. Especially Sartène. But it was Mérimée who made of Fozzano a permanent vendetta. When Carrington visited the town, soon after her arrival on the island, she was directed to Colomba's house by villagers who assured her it stood empty and was likely unlocked. She was able to let herself in, to sift through the debris in streaked light falling from the few, small windows. Even then she thought the town had been written by Mérimée, that the town made of words was at least as present as the town made of stones.

That was one hundred and ten years after the publication of *Colomba*. Sixty years on and Mérimée, if anything, dominates the town even more than before. Colomba's house, the tower, is now signposted twice; the newer placard identifies it as site #7 on an audio tour. As at Filitosa, modernity wants its scrim. But there was no one about to rent me a headset, and I wouldn't have had one anyway. The town was silent. The prospect blued by distance. I saw a woman peek from behind shutters, but I met no villagers. Perhaps, for literary travelers, they have in fact been expunged.

::

Mérimée arrived on Corsica drawn by the heat of its passions—not the vendetta, but what stood behind vendetta. It was a world where more was risked, where the unforgivable was always just there, at hand. And where, as Carrington puts it, "to accept forgiveness" was just "as humiliating as to offer it." It was a world where decisions were fatal. There is so much to deplore in this, no doubt. But we are in such a hurry to dismiss this way of living that we fail to consider its compensations. We fail to recognize that though we sit in appalled judgment on such behaviors, part of us understands the attractions quite well, and that's the part we take to the movies, that we indulge when we read crime fiction, especially *noir*, but so much of the imagined world has this fatal quality that you have to wonder why.

In old Corsica, not so long ago in places like Sartène, a girl's honor suffered if she was "seen speaking to an unrelated man, and lost if she [went] for a walk with him." If a man touched a woman's face or kissed her in a public place, he had to marry her immediately or face the knives of her relatives. The woman had no choice in the matter whatever—she had to marry the man or never marry, disgraced, whatever her feelings. Terrible, of course, especially for women. And yet it was a world where a kiss mattered, a glance, sweet words or hard words. It all mattered. The world was fatal. At bottom, I suppose, it still is, though we seem to be on the verge of forgetting it. Have we climbed or fallen into a world so easily dismissed with the word *whatever*? Sometimes seriousness itself seems to have gone lost.

It was cultural anemia that sent Mérimée and so many other nineteenth century writers to Corsica, a feeling of lassitude, the feeling that somehow nothing mattered as it should, and, even now, Corsica suggests a world with more felt gravity. If more abstractly. Not bloody vendetta, but the memory of it.

::

I sat at my jade-toped table watching a girl, a young woman, maybe. I'm old enough that it's hard for me to tell and surely doesn't matter. I'd seen her before, at a table in *La Victoire*, there with a large group, a family, bored it seemed. Now she was walking across *La Place* with a friend. She'd been in and out of the square several times since I'd been sitting there over a glass of chilled Sartène wine. I'd taken an interest. I'd begun to think I wanted her for a character. Her black hair in ringlets over her shoulders. Her slouchy, restless look. Her cutting eyes. A vaguely willful quality, both coltish and haughty. I thought she'd do. I scratched some notes on a receipt, and she was gone. When she unexpectedly crossed back into *La Place,* alone now, I stood up and followed her. I wanted to memorize her walk, which I noticed, walking behind her, was loose, a little uncoordinated, and her head swung about restlessly, looking this way and that as she turned down *Cours Soeur Amélie.* I dropped back. But a car door swung open blocking the sidewalk and she paused and suddenly I was only a few feet behind her. Her head came around and she looked at me, and something green shuddered through her gaze. I stopped. She had been going to wait for the car door to close, I think, but now she darted to the right, through the door of a small store that had connecting doors onto the next street, *Gabriel Peri*, which she must have taken, because quite all at once she was gone. When the sidewalk cleared I walked by the store, peered across toward the glazed door and windows, my gaze coming to rest finally on a plaque of sunlight hot on the tiled floor.

(2009)

TIME TO KILL: CAMBODIA

::

1.

He has looked down his road,
he is ready to go, not willingly
yet without useless resistance.
—Denise Levertov, "Stele"

The affair started with a smile, her smile. And as is so often the case in love, a smile not meant for me. The love was all on my side, but ardent, nevertheless. It's impossible love, after all, that tugs at us hardest. And that smile! Her face quiet, yet radiant, her eyes closed, as if she were listening to a sweet strain only she could hear. I wanted to hear it, too. Lips full, but delicate, her mouth closed, only at the corners a slight upturning, a responsiveness as if involuntary to something not amusing but good. As if she held a shelled almond on her tongue. As if she had understood that the secret was open and golden. Just there, if unspeakable. And as is also so often the case in love, I couldn't understand the indifference of others to that smile. They came and went, walked on by, the room full for a moment and then empty, except for me, still looking. Is it love that gives us eyes, understanding? Do we walk by glory every day, as if blind, failing to see, because our hearts are still? I think we do. And that's why we are lucky to be in love, whatever disasters love might bring in its train, and generally does. But I felt safe, this time, in my affections. The smile that held me, that radiance shed into the surrounding air, was not of flesh made but stone—the smile of a little Khmer goddess, on display in the Sackler Gallery in Washington, D.C. Whenever I was in town, I visited her there in that small room underground, under the Mall.

And then, one year I went back and she wasn't there. Maybe sent traveling or banished into storage, but gone. My heart ached, however ridiculous it sounds, jilted by a stone. All that gold feeling darkened down into the dull copper of an old penny. I looked around at the other ancient Khmer pieces, standing quietly on their white plinths. I could see the family resemblance, compassionate faces tempered by detachment. If it hadn't been for her face, her smile, I would have come away satisfied, feeling I knew a little more than before about how serenity can sweeten an expression. Instead, I came away hollow, like a man who has received dark tidings from afar. For all that, climbing the white stairs back up to ground level, I felt the beginning of a journey in my steps, that however long it might be deferred, I would be traveling to Cambodia, making a call on the Khmers. Years passed, but I didn't forget, and last May I made the trip.

I traveled wary, knowing my Khmer goddess was an old girl, going on a thousand years old. The fate of modern Khmers has been more a witness to how things can end than to how they last. It's hard to think of the Khmers now without tagging on *rouges*, that red the color of blood. Yet, studying pictures of contemporary Cambodia, of the low reliefs at Angkor Wat, even of Cambodia under Pol Pot, I thought I saw that smile everywhere, the one I'd first met on the little goddess in the Sackler. Traveling, I hoped to see it again.

::

2.

My hotel in Phnom Penh, the Indochine, faced the river, just across busy Sisowath Quay and a wide strip of green, a park along the riverbank. The surface of Tonlé Sap glittered in the sun, boats, small and large, seemed about to combust on its molten surface. Even in the heavy sun things were in motion out on the street, cyclos pedaling slowly by, a woman selling snails off a platform mounted on the handlebars of her bike, buzzing motorcycles, strolling touts. Man's smudge thick on everything. The walls of the Indochine had all been painted a dirty yellow, shiny, so they looked always wet. I wasn't sure if the place smelled like piss or if I was imagining it, if it was that yellow calling up the smell by way of association, but I wanted to be outside and spent as much time walking as possible, avoiding the sun on shadowed sidewalks, keeping my head under my white newsboy cap crossing streets. But long stretches in the open were daunting; jet lag and the baking heat conspired together to suggest sunstroke. Bending over a map of central Phnom Penh, I was struck by how much the layout of the streets looked like a spider web, radiating out from Psar Thmei, the central market (and indeed, the main market building does look a little like a monstrous, white spider, like something out of a cheap sci-fi movie).

On one of my walks I turned in at the National Museum, a place I'd been heading for ever since I climbed up the steps out of the Sackler, heart-hollow. Here for beauty, I found the National Museum building beautiful itself, the dusky rose walls of the pavilions, stuccoed columns, and the almost black, exposed teak ceilings and beams, all under a complicated red-tiled roof with sky tassels arcing up from the tip of every gable and rose spires poking at the sky. The galleries open on a central courtyard, there everything growing a glossy green. Flame trees. Blooming bougainvillea arbors beckoning with their leafy shade.

Even with Khmer sculptures only yards away, I had a hard time taking my eyes off the courtyard. But I did, I entered the galleries. And it was like a reunion of lovers in a far country. I found that face, that smile, four or five times. Faces so beautiful, so serene, they seemed somehow beyond the reach of grief and loss. They did not suggest denial, but an understanding deep enough that the worst and best of what we are lost their terrible attraction. A quiet place. I looked again and then sat down with a cold drink, content to be dazzled by the flickering light and lively shadows under the bougainvillea arbor, patches of light like gold koi teeming in murky water. People came and went. I watched three young monks out in the sun, by the fountain, children really, trying to retie their glowing orange and mustard robes. They seemed to be having difficulty, as if they didn't know how to make the yards of bright cotton behave.

Before I left, I lit three sticks of incense, poking them into a stone bowl full of sand in front of the statue that gripped me most tightly. Not the best preserved, charred and limbless, with a face that insisted on nothing, she did not assert or resist, but smiled. How I loved that smile!

Standing by the doorway, ready to go, I overheard a man in broken English ask a woman behind the ticket counter if it was true about the bats. *Yes*, was the answer, and that was how I found out that the museum, so beautiful, so elegant, had become over the years perhaps the most populous bat house on the face of the earth. Two million bats, maybe. Renovations had been required to shore up the ceilings under the accumulated weight of the guano, and to stop the drips. That had been done. Only after I knew they were there did I notice the thrum of the bats chittering and scratching overhead, in what must have been closely packed gables. Standing right there, I couldn't imagine those bats, the hot press of so much life so close. So I left, turned back to the streets of Phnom Penh.

::

146

3.

For days I walked, starting from the Indochine, along the river, and inland, away from the tourist blocks to dirt streets blackened by oil and exhaust, by small gasoline stands, a blue hand pump on wheels, to streets where more business was conducted under umbrellas than in the shoebox shops, where the poverty was obvious and the people looked tired of history. The scene was familiar, not so different than the busy *sois* of Bangkok or the 36 Streets of old Hanoi, but not quite like them, either. Here, the poor seemed listless, small commerce less energized. To get farther afield, I bargained for rides on the back of motorbikes, visited the Russian Market, and dropped in for caffeine at the swish Java Café, where the shiny optimism of the NGO expats seemed to have been ground down into knowing how to live well and cheaply in a dodgy place.

From the balcony, I looked out over the flat expanse of contemporary Phnom Penh, over the palm trees, thinking about the fall of the city to the Khmer Rouge in April of 1975, only thirty years back. The capital had been bursting with refugees, the population had ballooned from six hundred thousand to about two and a half million. The city did not please the Khmer Rouge leadership, who, making an implacable decision, ordered the citizens out. Anyone who would not, or could not leave at once was summarily shot, and the dispossessed millions were sent snaking out of the city with what little they could carry. Out on the road, without food or water, in the relentless heat of April, they died by thousands. That happened here, I told myself, and not here and there, but on every street in the city. Right there, on the sidewalk directly below my table. I wanted to accept this, however bitter the truth, but on my lips the knowledge tasted like poison. And the city had filled with people again, alive and wanting to live, walking the sidewalks however thick with shades. Phnom Penh is a young town, the great majority of the people living here were not even born in 1975. It is, of necessity, a new world now.

Wherever I walked in Phnom Penh, I was hailed by men on motos, men hoping to make a dollar taxiing tourists around the city. Open faced, they often seemed as interested in the chance to talk a little English as in the fare. Sometimes I was hot and said *yes*, and they'd tell me a story, their words riding the wind over their shoulder. More often than not, they spoke of the difficulties, of displacement and loss and working their way through school or looking for a job. Surprisingly few of these recitals ended in a plea for money. They were a people wanting to be heard. And sometimes I said *no* to the ride, preferring the slowness of walking, a pace that allowed me to see more. Often, this led to suggestions, of places the men on motorbikes thought I might want to go. The list was almost always headed by the torture chambers at Tuol Sleng or the Killing Fields. No one ever suggested the National Museum or even the Royal Palace with its Silver Pagoda. Tourists wanted to see the grim evidence, I didn't doubt it. After Angkor Wat, I wouldn't be surprised if Tuol Sleng and the Killing Fields aren't the most visited "sights" in the country. I certainly heard people talking about them—the before and after pictures, a lone red shoe, skulls, thousands of skulls. As in a myth, the earth sown with bones. I'd heard about the children playing with femur bones and tattered bits of clothing at the Killing Fields. Depravity exerts its own kind of fascination, shines with its own kind of dark energy. And it's to be hoped that controlled exposures inoculate. But I've had plenty, and I didn't feel like I needed a booster, so I stayed away.

Instead, I walked north along the riverfront one hot afternoon, looking for Wat Phnom, not hard to find as it occupies the only high ground in the city, a temple topping a small knoll like a gaudy hat. The grassy grounds are ringed by a roundabout, but the little hill looked terribly attractive as I approached it through the thick heat, green and tree shaded, the great *naga* staircase rising up before me, serpents for banisters. I must have already been climbing up, in my mind, my attention there on the stairs, not to have seen the first of the beggars approaching me. When I felt a tug on my sleeve, I glanced around at a little man hobbling beside me on a homemade crutch. Reaching into my back pocket, which I kept stuffed with Cambodian riel, I fished out a small note and gave it to him. It's shameful, I know, but handing him the money, I looked away, and in looking away I realized that this man was but an emissary, that a crippled nation was now struggling out of the shadows under the trees, struggling across the grass, converging on me. Perhaps they weren't so many, twelve or fifteen, but they suggested a vast suffering. They were the maimed, arms and hands, legs and feet blown away, faces erased by scars. Then they were pressing all around me. I reached into my pocket again and again, slipping a bill between outstretched elbows, into two-fingered hands. When they backed away, I climbed the steps alone, but occupied now by the maimed beggars, knowing already I'd have to find a way to live with these images.

After the Wat, I walked back down into Phnom Penh, crossing the roundabout and wading into what turned out to be the fortune-tellers' market: women reading cards or hands under bright pyramidal tents set out in neat rows under the widespread limbs of a great tree. I walked down the alleys, through sun and shade, the air blue with incense, followed first by a monkey and then by one of the wildest looking dogs I'd ever seen. Business was not brisk but steady, locals stopping in as matter-of-factly as they might to buy cigarettes or a loaf of bread. Customers sat down, got the news with bowed heads, paid and left. I found a bench and sat down myself, to watch the trade, wondering how good the news could be.

Late in the afternoon, walking back toward the Indochine along Tonlé Sap, my eyes were drawn to a tree near the river, shimmering, looking like it might be about to fly apart. At first I thought it was heat waves, but looking closer, I saw the tree was caught in a net of golden dragonflies. They were everywhere around it, in their thousands, but all close, within a foot or so of the tree's shiny leaves, and all in motion, a glowing web. Although I stood a long time staring, they were still there when I walked away.

::

4.

The Mekong Express bus crowded the skinny blacktop between Phnom Penh and Siem Reap, the pavement of Highway 6 not only narrow but pocked. I was on my way to Angkor Wat and the approach is through Siem Reap. Siem Reap for sleeping, for eating. An attractive town, if a tourist town, and quite international. I was on the bus to get there. Although Mekong Express buses are reputed to be the best public service going, they looked nothing like the sleek coaches of the private tours. Although not the only *farang* on the bus, almost all the other passengers looked to be middle-class Cambodians, including the dignified old fellow sitting next to me. Still, the service had pretensions; two girls in shiny dress uniforms patrolled the aisles and called out the sights over a microphone. One of them, dreamy faced, smiled quietly almost all the time, that smile I recognized. The bus ran through a number of market towns. At Skuon, I did see women and kids balancing bright tin platters of deep-fried spiders on their heads, a local delicacy, the spiders big enough to be eaten "like crabs." Our bus passed right on by, and just as well, as I was feeling disoriented enough without the spiders. The video system on the bus was playing a DVD over and over. The show opened with proud scenic shots of the ruins at Angkor Wat and then segued with dizzying speed to historical footage chronicling the rise of Pol Pot and the Khmer Rouge. The grim cadres, Pol Pot himself, his face serene, amiable, and the unstrung dead, so many. Then Angkor Wat again, a pink and purple sunrise, big music. Out of the corner of my eye I was watching the old man next to me; he would have been there for the mad times. He unwrapped his complimentary sandwich, ate it with circumspection, and drank a little bottled water. Although he was watching, his face betrayed nothing. It was as if I was seeing his face in deep shadow. But I felt relieved when one of the stewardesses removed the DVD in favor of an action movie.

I turned my attention to the landscape rolling by outside my window. The small towns looked dirty and depressed, but more surprising was the look of the country. I saw nothing of the careful cultivation of rice paddies and fields that make so much of agrarian Southeast Asia beautiful. In Thailand and Vietnam, even in Burma and Laos, the earth feels shaped by careful attention. Here, the land looked hacked at, by comparison only half tended. The farmers lived in sad thatched huts on stilts, huts without doors or windows, maybe a cow milling around a small compound or standing forlorn in a messy wallow out front. A few chickens scratching around in refuse left scattered about. The people seemed spellbound, slow moving if moving at all. A terrible lassitude seemed to have descended on the land, seemed to have mastered almost everyone. Perhaps it was the season, still dry in May; perhaps everyone was waiting for the rains, but it looked like there was work to do for the willing. I'm not a judgmental traveler, but the poverty outside my window looked miserable, the people not so much resigned as depressed. A woman's torso sprawled in a doorway, a baby lolling idly by her side. A boy standing knee deep in sludge, watching a cow trying to struggle out of a muddy wallow. A man sitting on the rough edge of a blackened haystack, hands on head, a blank expression on his face. A raggedy girl barefoot on a dirt path. A trussed up pig on the back of a motorcycle, feet treading the air.

Our big bus pulled into the station in Siem Reap more or less on time. The press of touts looked daunting enough from inside but when I stepped down onto the pavement I was just crushed by men and boys shouting out the name of a hotel or offering a ride. I made it down the side of the bus with difficulty, collecting my luggage in the escalating clamor. Then I was stuck. Several people tugged at my bag and the crowd pressed in tighter. By then it seemed like a mob, six deep all around me, everyone pushing to get close. I wasn't at all sure I could move if I wanted to, and I was glad to be tall enough to see over the scrum. Finally, putting aside my disinclination to shove, I bulled my way forward, toward a man standing by a motorcycle trailing a small cart, a kind of motorized cyclo. When I got to him I lifted my bag into the cart and jumped aboard, saying, Let's go. But by then there was no hurry; the crowd had loosened up, and I noticed several of the touts smiling: it was a game played for money but still a game.

::

5.

Siem Reap is not difficult, not hardly. In no time I'd settled in. It was easy to enjoy an evening stroll through lit streets, French Colonial architecture in pastel hues laid out for the most part on a neat grid. Every other building houses a restaurant; you could sit down to a different cuisine every night for a month here, or so it seems. Or Indian for a week and never twice in the same shop. Because I ate Cambodian most of the time, trying to get the taste of the place fixed in my mind, I settled on a small cafe a street back from the Old Market, tables under an awning running down an alley. That's where I sat, in the warm dark, watching, listening. A peaceful spot, children playing quietly, the low voices of walkers in town for the ruined temples of Angkor Wat, Japanese, Korean, French and English, German and more. And Khmer, of course. I ordered the amok, a fish curry thick with coconut milk, steamed and served in a banana leaf bowl. A Cambodian specialty, it tasted both pungent and mild, delicious. The name, maybe, is worrisome. Amok, to run amok, also, it seems, has been a Khmer specialty. If I couldn't taste it, my nose picked it up, like the burnt smell where a fire has run. I drank a little water, thinking about the madness. Then the waitress brought the bill and three rambutan in a small bowl, a little fruit by way of dessert. The husks were bright red and spiny; when I pulled them open they revealed the opaque fruit, smooth, encasing a large stone. Sweet, the texture like fresh lychee or a very ripe persimmon.

Walking to my hotel, the Golden Temple, I passed through the night world, a world of whispered suggestions from men dusky in the shadows, of strident streetwalkers waving at cars on Sivatha. Here, as in Phnom Penh, many reel in the night, stumbling toward stupor, it seemed to me. The Golden Temple was at the end of a dark alley, lit only by windows and the occasional open shop, low lanterns hanging from trees to illuminate a grill, a tray of grasshoppers or beetles, an array of fruit. Hands in a circle of light under shadowed faces. I walked warily, keeping to the center of the dirt road. Everywhere a world for sale. Outside the gate of the Golden Temple, I stopped to talk to a man on a Honda Dream trailing a buggy. I take tourists out to Angkor, he said, showing me his licenses. I liked him, so we chatted about his rates, and when he understood I was alone and planning to spend a week in the ruins he offered me a good price, and we struck a deal.

I hadn't been expecting it, but the next day began with a call to prayer, the loud, amplified voice of a muezzin swimming out of the black air when I was still sleeping. Cham Muslims, I surmised, eyes closed, no doubt themselves still trying to slough off the nightmare of the Khmer Rouge, who had singled them out for especially bad treatment when the atrocities were general. The call to prayer, ever so sweetly sung.

Sotheara was waiting when I emerged from the hotel courtyard; he chattered patiently as I got myself arranged under the buggy's low hood. Then he started the Dream, and we rolled out into the morning traffic. The road to Angkor Wat was busy. The temples are touristed, I'd been advised, so I encouraged Sotheara to visit temples between the tour busses. He knew their schedules, and in our week in the ruins he kept me out of the crowds. Indeed, often I had the temples pretty much to myself. And it is temples, plural. The name Angkor Wat refers to a particular temple complex, as well as to all the temples in the region, a lot of them. While most of the ruins are concentrated in the vicinity of Angkor Wat proper, there are outliers, the gorgeous Banteay Srei and the early temples known as The Rolous Group among them. Angkoran construction took place from the ninth to the early fourteenth century, a period in which the power of the Khmers waxed and waned more than once. Hinduism and Buddhism, according to the faith of the Kings, found favor and intertwined. The ruins at Angkor are what's left—a fraction—of what was constructed in stone; what was built in wood—by far the greater part—is all gone. A tourist, poking at stones, never gets closer than an inkling of the whole. But the ruins speak loudly, nevertheless, right now; Angkor Wat appeals not only to tourists from abroad; it's also a pilgrimage site for Khmers in the twenty-first century. As it was for the Khmer Rouge, who did not dare deface these places, however much havoc they wrought elsewhere. Indeed, they tried to graft the bright aura of the Angkoran kingdoms onto their own black souls.

::

6.

I went to the ruins in a comic little buggy, Sotheara on his Honda Dream in front of me. Early every day we passed by the great moat that surrounds Angkor Wat proper, two hundred yards wide, running almost a mile on each of its sides, the clutch of five towers on the temple mountain jutting over the low horizon at the heart of the complex: Mount Meru, home to gods. And Khmers fishing in the moat, bathing, the water golden in the slant light, studded here and there by a solitary lotus flower erect on its stem. Where the road parallels the moat, vendors set up everywhere, as if the circus came to town every morning here, and indeed you might see elephants, though the elephant parking lot lies just beyond Angkor Wat, immediately in front of the great south gate of Angkor Thom, where tall tour buses pass under the watchful eyes of a high tower adorned on all four sides by a serene face, a guardian presence. Angkor Thom, the walled city, was home to about a million people early in the thirteenth century, when the great capitals of Europe were by comparison mere towns. But I am not the one to fix the place of Angkor Wat in the plaited braids of cultural history, nor even the one to describe the ruins knowingly, as an archaeologist or an art historian might. I'm just the guy still trying to respond to a thousand-year-old smile, myself caught in an oddball web of associations here at my desk. Still, I was avid for the beauty of the stones at Angkor; in a week I visited twenty-nine temples, slowly, patient in my attentions. Some called me back, and I visited them more than once. I found that smile I was looking for, over and again, and my heart cracked. I found it on the face of Buddha, on gods and goddesses, on the *aspara* dancers. I found it on the faces of children, on the boy who offered to drink the rest of my Coke when I put it down, on little girls selling whatever they were selling, the innocents, many of them destined to be beer girls or worse in Siem Reap, no doubt, and soon. Hadn't I seen their sisters there at night, faces painted thick as masks?

At the end of a day in the ruins, I would retire to a shady place, literally stunned, my eyes heavy and aching in my head, phosphorescing. Rarely have I experienced such a daunting sun, a sensible pulse in the air and bounding up off the stones like radiation. My own white shirts and hat, picked to be cool, reflected the light back into the humid air around me; in the sun I could feel myself glowing, like a light bulb.

::

7.

The cosmological architecture at Angkor Wat surprised me in being so rectilinear. Most architecture, of course, is rectilinear, but the ruins at Angkor insist on it, probably because they are also severely symmetrical. What's on the right has its mirror image in what's on the left. So much order can be oppressive, but for the most part it didn't feel that way. The symmetry was softened by ruin, the stones worn or gone, and strangely, by the sheer scale of these places. Sometimes the symmetries were almost too big to be noticed. And oddly enough, the heavy light could make even the same thing look different. The shadows were heavy, too; I suppose the explanation must lie in the eye's response to all that sun. But to step inside was to step into a shadowland, into darkness strung with cobwebs.

In those complexes where the big trees of the surrounding jungle have been allowed to stand, in Ta Prohm and Preah Khan, the symmetry of the temples is both accentuated and diminished by the sinuosity of the big trees, the strangler figs and kapoc trees. The incursions of the great figs at Ta Prohm are often called romantic, but the effect is stronger than that, otherworldly. Under a green canopy, the pale roots have run riot, as if the trees were monstrous tallow tapers that had streamed rivulets of wax over the ruins, many of the roots broad as a large man and twenty or thirty feet long. The stones of these temples are clutched, smothered by the roots' too-tight embrace. Hence the name strangler fig, I imagine, but then how unsettling, even unseemly, that its Latin name should be *ficus religiosa*, and that the bo tree the determined Siddhartha sat down to meditate under, once, long ago in India, was just such a tree.

But it's the long walls of low reliefs that most keep pilgrims from feeling imprisoned by the massive, rectilinear architecture at Angkor Wat. There must be miles of carved stone, many miles, the living gods enlivening what would otherwise be blank with their epic struggles; and Khmer kings; and common men and women going about their lives. It's hard, in looking, not to forget where you are, to remember that what you're looking at is a small part of something else; the carved stone is so arresting that everywhere the big plan disappears behind your attention to detail. The low reliefs are so many, so extensive, that even a list of the most famous would run for pages. The multi-tiered panels in the outer galleries at Bayon? The incredible liveliness, the surpassing beauty of the carving at Banteay Srei? The thousands of *apsara* dancers at Angkor Wat proper? They beggar description. And I think somehow the sheer number of sculpted forms itself is part of the meaning, that in their profusion there is a suggestion about how all living things pour together into being, radiant and shadowed alike. We're all dancing at the same party, and for all our going forever renewed.

A guy can get dizzy glowing in the sun, and stepping into deep shade at Angkor Wat often makes for strange meetings. A bat disturbed by my entry winging away down a stone corridor. The surprise at seeing a beautiful face over my shoulder, that smile; it wasn't just another goddess carved in stone. For a moment, I was really alive to what was there. I'd been opened by beauty. Then, walking through the jungle on the long approach to Preah Khan, I stopped to listen to the music, the sound of traditional Khmer instruments played by a Victims of Landmines Band. I sat down on a log between two monks who were also listening, the performance lively, good, in spite of the prosthetics. No member of the band was whole in body. I had come to accept the many maimed of Cambodia; wherever I ate in Siem Reap, it seemed, a man with his arms blown off above the elbows would find me and I'd pay up, glad finally to be able to. He was there, I'd learned to see the man in his eyes. Or the legless fellow on his little cart. If I didn't notice him he tugged at my pant leg. We had come to an understanding.

The sex tourists proved harder to accept, finally. Especially one I saw too often at my hotel, a young westerner, a man wearing the sick smirk of a hyena, always escorting around some confused-looking Khmer girl. One morning, I saw him loitering in the lobby with two, one sitting quietly in a chair with a large stuffed animal on her lap. This punk I wanted to slap around, and I didn't like feeling the red pulse of violence, the adrenaline rushing through my veins.

::

8.

One day Sotheara took me out to the Roluos group, three ninth century temples about ten miles east of Siem Reap. Perhaps I was getting tired, because at Bakong, after walking the causeway across the moat, my attention was diverted by the modern Wat off to the right. Modern, that is, compared to the ruins, but the main temple in the compound must have been quite old; the tile roof had long been discolored by the weather. The building itself had the most elaborate paint job imaginable, ochers and a purplish blue, green columns, red, a lot of red. And almost every available surface had been painted in frescoes, scenes from the life of the Buddha and wild creatures spawned out of the deep unconscious mind or myth. I passed through a wicket and stood in the courtyard, agog, really, but wondering about the great guardian figures painted on the lintels, each one gnashing a sword in its teeth: there to keep the place safe. Against the Khmer Rouge they had not prevailed; the monks were slaughtered all over the country, their bloody mustard and orange robes thrown up into the trees as a sign. One book I read said of the 60,000 monks living in Cambodia when the Khmer Rouge took power, 59,000 were dead three and a half years later at the fall of the regime (and the cadres held parts of the country for almost two decades after that). Nothing speaks to the ambitions of the Khmer Rouge quite so forcibly as the slaughter of the monks in Cambodia. Pol Pot meant to kill the culture, nothing less, and in a culture as thoroughly infused with Buddhism as Cambodia's, there was no better place to start the killing than with the monks. And the longer I was in Cambodia the more I realized that the Khmer Rouge had succeeded to an extent I didn't want to believe. They killed the teachers, the doctors, the dancers, the artists, anyone who wore glasses. . . Although once again there are many monks in Cambodia, the great continuity of learning seems to have been broken down. Somehow the culture feels thin. The wats in Laos and Thailand, even in Burma, hum with activity, the old ripening the young. But in Cambodia, the wats seem to have fallen under a spell; things are eerily quiet; at some wats the only monks I saw were children.

Sometimes between temples I ate in one of the makeshift restaurants near the Terrace of the Elephants in Angkor Thom. Sotheara teaches English for free to the children working in these places, and while we ate the kids stopped by to chatter and smile. At my prompting, Sotheara told me how he had ended up on a Honda Dream. His grandfather had been a provincial governor, his father a doctor in his hometown. When Pol Pot came to power Sotheara's father took the family into hiding; they moved to a town on the Thai border, and Sotheara's father passed himself off as a farm laborer. They lost everything, but they lived. The grandfather, who refused to believe how dire the situation had become, stayed behind and was one of the first of the villagers killed when the Khmer Rouge took power. The murderer still lives in the village. Everybody knows what he did, Sotheara said. When Sotheara grew up he wanted to go back, to kill the man who had killed his grandfather, but his own father wouldn't let him. It's all karma, his father said. The story is not extraordinary; almost without exception the killers have not been brought to justice. They are there, and I think sometimes I saw them, dead or demonic faces that scared me. They must be very many—hundreds of thousands of Cambodians were executed by the Khmer Rouge and, including disease and famine, perhaps two million died (estimates vary wildly). Few if any could have escaped a particular grief, and the common grief was—is— overwhelming. Here the shades crowd around the living, beseeching. Most Cambodians must live half among the clamoring dead.

::

9.

Before I left Siem Reap, Sotheara took me back to Angkor Wat proper for a last visit. I went to look, first and last, at the *apsara* dancers, to see again the smile that had called me to this place. There are about two thousand low relief dancers at Angkor Wat, and hundreds of them know to smile in that way that consoles me. While it's not difficult to observe repeats in the fantastic hairdos, jewelry, and clothes, the *apsaras* seem each a particular someone. Celestial nymphs churned out of a sea of milk by the divine Vishnu, who employed for the job on one hand the benevolent *devas*, and on the other the malevolent *asuras*, gods all. It was a divine tug of war, the *devas* pulling on one end, the *asuras* on the other end of a giant *naga*, which turned the churn. And like butter, out of the milk, the *apsaras* emerged, dancing, their faces bright from the beginning with an ageless smile.

I walked in sun, I walked in shadow, I looked into the faces of the *apsaras*. Many were eroded, many restored, and a few pocked by bullets, where someone had turned a gun on beauty. Even about this, the dancers are indifferent. They do what they can, they dance.

Soon thereafter I took the bus back to Phnom Penh and then from the capital traveled by taxi on down to Kampot to see the colonial architecture the French abandoned there when they left. I went by motorbike on to the beach at Kep and in the back of a pickup truck up through Bokor National Park to the old French hill station at about 3,500 feet. Clouds of butterflies roiled the air as we passed through the jungle on Bokor, a place wild enough. The view from behind the shell of Bokor Palace, over a precipice, over jungle and then islands to the Gulf of Thailand, was like gazing into an opal the day I was there, so mixed were the colors of cloud and sky, sea and trees. And I was lucky enough to see a brown and yellow hornbill, his head white and luminous, a magical bird, riding the thermals like an eagle just below my feet.

But by the time I got back down to the bottom of the mountain, had floated back into Kampot town on the silky skin of the Tek Chou river, I was longing for home. The Khmer Rouge held on in Kampot province until the mid '90s, and a great many of them have settled in; I'd seen more demonic faces here than anywhere else in Cambodia, and I didn't like harboring suspicions. Enough, I thought, and I began to arrange for my departure.

::

10.

Back in the States, I found myself ill at ease, somehow unsettled by where I had been. Cambodia, I said, when asked, but I didn't try to explain the difficulty I was having feeling at home at home, perhaps because the experience wasn't entirely novel; I have often had more difficulty with culture shock returning from long trips than in going. When friends stopped by, I often volunteered to queue up a slideshow on my laptop of pictures I'd taken in Cambodia, a behavior so uncharacteristic of me that I could hardly identify the guy asking, Would you like to see some photos? Standing there, looking over the shoulder of a friend, I was simply dumbfounded to see the world I'd photographed, the seamless beauty of the place. I wanted to object, to insist there was something wrong with the shots. But I didn't, I didn't know exactly what to say. Instead, I offered to print a copy of whatever picture my friend liked best. Nicole chose an *apsara* dancer, one not so beautiful nor serene, but joyous, a bird or a lotus blossom rising from her hand. When I picked it out of the printer tray, I was surprised to see the tattered web of an orb spider, not noticed on the laptop's screen, draped all across her face and body, and studded with dead insects. Somehow it seemed a better picture of where I'd been, and I was pleased that when I asked Nicole if she'd like to pick again she said *no*.

::

11.

*She too accepts the truth, there is no way back,
but she has not looked, yet, at the path
accorded to her. She has not given herself,
not yet, to her shadowhood.*
     —Denise Levertov, "Stele"

I expected to get over it, for Cambodia to settle in among the other places I have traveled, and behave. That it didn't surprised me, but I couldn't deny that I felt uneasy, anxiety ever at my elbow. I felt like I had sustained a wound in Cambodia, though there was nothing I could point to, nothing traumatic had happened, nothing at all. For all that, I felt like I needed to be healed, that I was hemorrhaging inside. One night, months on, I had a dream. If the dream didn't heal me, perhaps it did speak to the nature of my wound. In the dream, I found myself imprisoned in the jungle, in a rough stockade made of peeled logs lashed together with wire or vines. I was not alone, there were twenty or thirty other men penned in with me, Cambodians, but I didn't register any difference betweeen them and me. I was one of them. Somehow I was both in my body behind the stockade wall and at the same time floating a ways above it, and outside the enclosure I could see Pol Pot chatting ever so casually with the camp commander, deciding, as if it was a matter of no particular importance, or even interest, that we prisoners should die. I looked up into the green canopy out of a deep shade. Immediately a door opened in the prison wall and a Khmer Rouge soldier handed in a couple of plastic bottles, the jugs white like Clorox bottles but with the top cut away just above the handle. The jugs went round. In the dream, I noticed the grimy feel of the dirt on the handle when the poison got to me. I looked inside the opened throat of the jug into darkness. Then, without much thinking, I lifted it to my lips. I was resigned, that's all, to dying. I had time to hand the jug along to the next man before I felt the burning in my throat and the first convulsive shudder. Then I woke up, shaken to understand that in such a place I would just let go of living. The thing is, I don't believe that dream was just mine. I think that dream was common.

(2007)

A HOUSE FITTING

::

The man with his hands on the grips was Nyoman; the big motorcycle rumbled at his suggestion then bolted forward. I was the other guy, the guy on the back, just along for the ride. We leaned into the corner at Ubud Palace and swept by the crowd of cars-for-hire clustered there. Nyoman made short work of the blocks of restaurants and shops, the guesthouses; then, we were out in the country, rising up through terraced rice fields, the flooded paddies reflecting a heavy, silver light. Things looked to be getting agrarian, but not entirely. Right-in-the-rice-fields appeals to tourists, so guesthouses and villas often intrude on the farming life. Bali has been a spoiled paradise for a very long time, at least for those who want to be the only fallen Adam or Eve in sight. But long ago I fell hard and far, and I no longer expect the world to come to me all clean.

I looked over Nyoman's shoulder, my face turned to the rush of palms against a mottled blue sky, white egrets over the sharp green of new shoots of rice. Bougainvillea and paradise banana. Clumps of deep yellow coconuts and the solid promise of green papayas. Kinds of bamboo. The small, tended shrines to Dewi Sri, the rice goddess. The place looked good to me! And passing.

Nyoman powered down and braked to a stop on a graveled berm. He nodded toward a gate as I swung off the back then pulled the big machine up on its stand. He flashed his loopy grin, just like when he'd told me he used to be cool. Now he is warm, friendly. He was the second person I'd shook hands with on Bali. His name had given me a little shock when I first met him. The taxi driver who'd brought me out from Denpasar had also introduced himself as Nyoman. What are the chances of that? I'd thought. Pretty good, as it turns out. Children in Bali are named according to birth order, male or female (gender noted only by an article): Wayan, Made, Nyoman, Ketut. After four, the names cycle through the list again. My original sense of unlikely coincidence had given way before a greater doubt. The Balinese way of naming got me thinking, about what they do, and about what we do, how we give given names. The best travel estranges in just this way—insists our worlds are made up. Which is not to say arbitrary. Different worlds don't cancel each other out, don't make it all relative and meaningless. Everything human speaks. But sometimes at home the world speaks in a drone, the familiar drowns out the strangeness of our own choices.

All of which sounds terribly abstract. The abstraction is in thinking about it, but before the thinking there is a moment when the flatness of things seems to go 3D. Just seeing. And that moment, densely suggestive, feels valuable, whether or not the suggestions are ever taken up.

I stepped through the gate ahead of Nyoman. He'd asked me if I was interested in seeing the place, a new villa he'd built recently, and I'd said sure. Perhaps he'd hoped I'd be so taken with it I'd want to rent the place, if not now, another time. And maybe he was a little proud of it. I did like it. For new construction, it had surprising presence, perhaps because in Bali the new begins to look old very quickly. Still, I liked my place in town at Nyoman's homestay better, where I could walk almost anywhere in Ubud. I had a second-floor room overlooking the family compound, which was full of flowering trees and birds, some wild and some caged. Besides, the address could not be improved upon, the place was called Nirvana, the street, Goutama. And it was much cheaper than the villa.

Walking back to the motorcycle, Nyoman, who in his cool days had adopted the nickname Yoyo, after the toy, mentioned that the villa had been built *asta kosala kosali*, according to the old ways. That explains the feel of the place, he said, pushing his oversize horn-rimmed dark glasses back up the bridge of his nose, Good, no? He straddled the big motorcycle, his batik sarong pulled taut over his thighs. I got on the back, peering one last time at the compound's heavy great gate. It looked overbuilt; you walked under as well as through it, and you felt the change going in and coming out.

On the ride back into town, it occurred to me that if I had been born Balinese I would have been named Nyoman, too. The way identity sticks to a name seemed, for a second, to pull loose; then I was Kevin again, paying closer attention to the thick, roofed gates that lined the road than I had on the ride out. The variety was daunting—stone or wood, brick or mud—and yet, even sweeping by, there seemed to be a family resemblance, a common feeling that joined them all. Not surprisingly, it was with gates, doors, that I started to take an interest in traditional Balinese architecture. I hadn't been inside much. It was my first time on Bali, and I had no sooner arrived than I'd fallen under the spell of Balinese dance. If I wasn't at a performance, I soon would be. So most of the architecture I saw was public or sacred; Ubud Palace hosted dances regularly, as did any number of community halls and Hindu temples in the region.

Nyoman, no doubt noticing my developing mania, began to suggest dance performances that would not otherwise have come to my attention. He sent me to school, to watch children learning to dance. He sent me to see pendet as it was meant to be danced, in a temple, in Peliatan. I watched gambuh at a major temple rededication in Kedewatan. And one night, he arranged for me to see Christine Formaggia and her small troupe dance topeng in a Brahmin temple I don't know where, somewhere down a lot of twisty roads. Topeng is danced masked, a few dancers taking many parts in an old court story. The dancers assumed a new identity every time they put on a different mask, and the performance stretched for hours. That night was the only time I saw traditional topeng, though often public dance performances included one or another topeng character dancing solo, generally the old man, an odd choice. Somehow I ended up in the back seat of Christine's own beat-up station wagon for the ride back to Ubud. She drove badly and that car had no springs, I swear. Still, I was amused until she dumped me out at the bridge in Campuhan and I was left to walk back to Nirvana at that hour when the gates are all closed and the Bali dogs get threatening. I began to see myself as a figure of fun, ridiculous in my obsession with Balinese dance. It wasn't even a big obsession, nothing like the tragedy of the grand balletomanes throwing their fortunes and reputations at the feet of some willowy girl. No, I was just the guy who showed up early to sit in the front row, mildly besotted.

So I pulled back and began to notice the architecture. By the time I left Bali I had a sense of the vocabulary of Balinese building, and I thought I could tell the difference between buildings that were "Bali style" and buildings that were more traditionally Balinese. But I had no idea how conditioned my responses were by the categories I brought to what I was seeing. My understanding was almost entirely aesthetic and/

or functional. Back home, I started to read. Immediately I found myself revising what I thought I'd seen, and, soon thereafter, planning another trip.

::

I wanted to get myself measured for a house. It sounds odd, I know. And when I got back to Bali, it played as odd there, too, because I wasn't interested in actually building. I just wanted to speculate a house, imagine up a house compound that would be, in the Balinese way, right for me. To have my measure taken, literally. Because the first thing I discovered was that the traditional Balinese compound is sized to its owner, to his body rather than to the size of his pocket book. This fitting is not only general, a big house for a big man, but particular and thoroughgoing. The body of man, a man, becomes the measuring stick for the construction of his family's compound. (Always a man? The structure of traditional Balinese society seems to make no provision for women in this regard, though I see no reason why a woman's body could not function in just the same way—as a ruler.)

Man is the measure of all things, here, not in the Protagorean sense, but quite literally. I read all about it, how thin strips of bamboo were notched according to the size of various spans on the body, and how the strips of bamboo then became the rulers used in construction—without the mediation of any other system of measurement. Nothing like inches, feet, or yards, just notches on a bamboo stick (called a *gagulak*). I had no sooner understood this than I wanted one of those sticks. My stick, my ruler. A sad, self-regarding desire, perhaps, but there you have it.

Of course, I already had some sizes. 6'. A weight (variable). 12, for shoes. 7¾, for hats. 45, for a jacket. Large. And once as a young man—what was I thinking?—I'd even got myself measured for a suit. It'll wear like iron, was what the salesman said.

One size never fits all, of course, but what the Balinese way seemed to suggest was that size was not an external measure at all, to be fit into, but something inherent, something that could be made manifest. And, through *asta kosala kosali*, seen, inhabited.

When I read the term, which refers to the whole practice of traditional architecture in Bali, I remembered having heard it drop from Nyoman's lips when we inspected his new villa outside Ubud. Although clearly not an entirely traditional compound, even in memory I recognized the expansive feel of that place as an extension of Nyoman's own considerable amplitude. He's a big guy, by Balinese standards, a very big guy. When he rides his motorcycle through the streets of Ubud, shining black hair tied in a batik kerchief, often wearing a canvas vest, he's not mistaken for anybody else. What Nyoman called the good feel of his villa, of buildings constructed according to the *lontars* of *asta kosala kosali*, however, derives not so much from size as from layout and proportion, though a small man's compound would be constructed along less generous lines. A balanced beauty, deep in the bones of how a compound is conceived. A westerner, likely, assimilates the effect to aesthetics, if not anthropology. But the builders, and indeed Balinese in general, while alive to aesthetic effects, arrive at them through indirection. Their aims are broadly religious rather than aesthetic. And perhaps beauty is more amenable to an oblique than to a direct approach. Like happiness. Happy people don't pursue it. They live well, live in a world of felt meanings, and find that they are happy. To act for happiness is to live in a whirlpool of self-regard, which promotes not happiness but despair. Or so I was thinking, trying to understand why beauty should so often appear where it is not looked for, in the living, and why it often evades those who self-consciously set out to have it.

::

So I returned to Bali. Again the great dome of blue sky, the flowering, the milk-and-butter colors of frangipani, painted beauties, like hibiscus and flame trees. When I stepped out of the taxi, it all came rushing back. The alley dogs on Goutama seemed to know me—they couldn't be bothered to raise a racket. I rolled my bag down the long cobbled walkway to Nirvana, the feeling of return strong within me. I passed through the compound gate into the courtyard and there sat Nyoman, deep in a book. Then he raised his head and gave me his loopy grin and said, You're back, welcome, not surprised at all. He called for the houseboys to carry a writing table up into my old room. The cockatiels roused themselves, and a new bird, a vivid lori, showed off a little, turning on his perch, well satisfied, apparently, with his coat of many colors.

Although I intended to have my measure taken soon after I returned to Ubud, and did give my attention to vernacular housing whenever I went walking, by night I found myself again in thrall to the dance. I found I was seeing it differently, more the dancer than the dance. Perhaps I was inching closer to the role of the dance-drunk balletomane.

Days, then weeks passed. Everything felt as if it had happened between dances, and it had, but getting measured for a house hadn't happened at all. I had applied to Nyoman, of course, thinking he'd be able to put me in touch with an architect conversant with *asta kosala kosali*. But the architects he knew charged a hundred dollars an hour and built Bali-style internationally, houses that were more about a look than a tradition. Young architects speaking fluent English, that was the attraction, but also the problem. Slowly it dawned on me that one of their kind was not likely to be an *undagi*, a traditional Balinese architect. And I thought too that perhaps the measure of my wallet had been mistaken.

I often stopped in my walking about to talk with Madé, a driver who had his stand at the corner of Goutama and Jalan Raya. Last year he'd helped me find my way into the studio of one of the best traditional painters in Bali, in Kamasan, translating my many questions. When I asked Made if he could put me in touch with an *undagi*, he said he knew an architect in the village next to his own. His cousin, as a matter of fact.

Made suggested his cousin while he was negotiating the narrow bridge over the river at Campuhan. Then we swung right, heading up the hill toward Neka Museum. He was working, an Australian girl in the back paying the fare on a ride to a meditation center away from the noise of town. Made asked me to explain again what I wanted, having some difficulty getting it, in spite of his more than serviceable English. He repeated what I'd said back to me, then gave me a blank look, his eyes round. I had started in again when the girl in the back leaned forward between the seats; she said, to Made, Pretend, he wants to pretend!

Then we were there and the girl got out and Made asked me to explain the whole thing one more time, and I did, stressing that I would want my own bamboo rulers, notched in the old way, according to the measure of my body. Finally, Made nodded, fished a cell phone out of his shirt pocket, and called his cousin. His explanation of what I wanted was punctuated by a good deal of laughing, I noticed, but the cousin agreed to humor me and a time was agreed on.

::

Although it's not immediately apparent in a town like Ubud—by now an amalgam of several villages—a traditional Balinese village is laid out on an axis, the orientation of which is determined by how the village sits in the landscape. The cardinal directions are *kaja*, mountainward, and *kelod*, seaward; so a village on the north side of the island has, according to the compass, an orientation that reverses the orientation of a village in the south. But that's a western view. For the Balinese, all traditional villages have the same orientation, which turns around—like spokes in a wheel— the axel of Gunung Agung, the mountain residence of the gods. Seaward is always away from the mountain, as the sea is all around.

If *kaja* is the direction of the sacred, *kelod* is the direction of the profane. The people live in between. The axis of life itself is made manifest in the placement of a traditional village's three principal temples: *pura puseh*, the temple of origin, is sited mountainward; *pura desa*, the main temple, stands at the center of the town; while seaward lies *pura dalem*, sometimes called the temple of the dead, with its burning ground and attendant cemetery. The Balinese worship Wishnu at *pura puseh*, Brahma at *pura desa*, and Siwa at *pura dalem*. The layout of the village thus mirrors the cosmological structure of the universe, which suggests a way of seeing things quite different than what we mean by city planning.

But the Balinese did not exhaust their cosmological zoning of the "built structure" of their world in the orientation of the village; each temple exhibits the same *kaja/kelod* orientation, as do traditional house compounds, where the family temple occupies the most sacred corner of the grounds, while in the most profane corner animals mill in their pens by the garbage pit.

Corner, rather than end. Because in addition to the primacy of what is mountainward and what is seaward, the Balinese understanding of space is also conditioned by what is eastward, toward the rising sun, and what is westward, toward the setting sun. Eastward, *kangin*, is the second most sacred direction, while westward, *kauh*, is the second least.

Kangin and *kauh* remain constant all over the island, but how they align with *kaja* and *kelod* varies depending on where you are in relation to Gunung Agung. Which makes for complexity. The zoning of space is layered. Transparencies would help. But, really, you're going to need an *undagi* to sort out the difficulties when it comes time to build.

The Balinese organization of space is both stunningly abstract and remarkably visual. So near the equator, the sun rises in the west all year round. You can look—*kangin*. And *kaja* is not known by faith— on clear days the blue profile of the big mountain shows, unmistakably, there. On cloudy days, you have the evidence of the architecture, if you know how to read it. But you can't see just how pervasive the Balinese sense of direction is in consciousness, how meaningful. The westerner's sense of direction is not only depressed but, by now, almost meaningless. It's a W on a freeway sign, little more. "Going westward," in the old Irish sense, calls for a footnote. For most westerners, a significant sense of direction is now so lost it's not even missed. Our orientation has more to do with where we want to get to than where we actually are.

In Bali, when a man lies down to sleep he points his feet seaward, *kelod,* or westward, *kauh.* He knows which way. The body too is zoned, the head sacred, the feet profane, the trunk between. Standing, the head is up, and in that sense mountainward, the feet down, seaward, a physical relation that's maintained while sleeping by orienting the body *kaja-kelod,* or *kangin-kauh.*

By the time I returned to my bed at Nirvana a second year, I knew enough to realize that the headboard was *kelod,* that in the dark under my mosquito net I slept, somehow, upside down, like a bat in a cave.

::

Made's blue van squeezed around a parked car on Goutama before rolling to a stop. Body a bit battered, creaking in the springs, an engine that pinged—old. I climbed in what felt to me like the wrong door—Bali being one of those places where cars come with a right-hand drive. And small—I sat with my knees pressed against the dash for the duration. But Made's cousin's village came up quick; not far from Ubud, it had none of Ubud's flashiness. No tourists, nothing for tourists. No shops, no signs. A face without make-up. The three temples, community buildings, a drum tower. The plain walls of modest house compounds. And then we were there.

After the introductions, we settled down on the mats in the guest pavilion (*bale*). Made introduced his cousin, Wayan, not a traditional *undagi* but a university educated architect who had studied the old ways at school. Another cousin, Ketut, soon joined us, a builder. Ketut's wife brought out soft drinks, and before long there was quite a crowd come to see the westerner with the weird request. Again, I explained what I wanted. An old man shuffled up and the cousins translated for him. I could hardly take my eyes off the old fellow, stately in his batik sarong and twist of a hat. When I asked who he was, he cocked his head, his brown eyes sympathetic, as Made explained that he was their grandfather, who had himself been a builder of traditional houses his whole working life. Now well into his eighties, he slept in a tiny *bale* a few steps across the open court from where we were sitting. It looked to be the oldest structure in the compound, the *bale dangin*, or ceremonial pavilion. The old man, a Wayan too, preferred to sleep out of doors, and made up his bed on the platform that hung directly from the teak corner posts, the very place his corpse would be laid out when that day arrived. I asked if old Wayan's was the body that had been measured when the *bale dangin* was built, but the pavilion was older than that even, over a hundred years old.

I was ready, ready for my body to manifest its proportions into space, for my place to take shape, if only in imagination, under the afternoon sun, light pouring from the west. And out came the tape measure. *Gagulaks?* I asked. The architect gave me a puzzled look, holding up the tape. Bamboo *gagulaks?* Only old Wayan nodded. But clearly no bamboo strips had been prepared. I glanced at Made and he glanced at the architect. They talked. Finally, Made said, Same, same. I thought it made a difference, that to notch a *gagulak* was not the same thing as referring everything to an external measure. But I didn't insist; I didn't see how insisting would help.

Depa, asta, musti, old Wayan said suddenly, forcefully. Then he showed me, first pointing to the tips of his middle fingers, he stretched his arms out, as wide as they would go, *Depa. Asta*, he said, reaching his right arm out in front of him, he touched his elbow, then lifted his forearm up, indicating the tip of his extended middle finger. *Asta*, he said again. Then he held up a fist, and pointed at the span between the bottom of his little finger and the top of his thumb, *Musti. Depa, asta, musti*, the old man chanted, demonstrating the spans one after another as if he was doing Tai Chi or perhaps signaling the pilot of a jet, maneuvering a big plane up to the terminal. The old man's outsize gestures pulled *asta kosala kosali* out of the books for me, made the living current in the traditional ways hum. I felt the body in the measure. A traditional *undagi* would have notched my *depa asta musti* onto a *gagulak*, and it would have been used to lay out the *bale* walls.

We started in. They measured the length of my foot, the *tampak*, 29 centimeters, and the width, the *urip*, 10 centimeters. They showed me how to pace off, heel to toe, the various spans in a house compound.

The distances were always a significant multiple of the length of my foot, with the addition of a single width (the *urip*). Although a compound would be conditioned by the owner's caste, wealth, the size of the family, and the desired level of embellishment, the placement of the *bales* within the compound would always be measured out by the owner's feet. My feet struck the little crowd gathered around to watch the proceedings as amusingly large. Indeed, every single part of me occasioned a snicker as too big. The pavilions that rose up in their imaginations as we worked through the most important measurements must have been so outsize as to seem almost grotesque. As a person, I was overbuilt.

The most striking feature of Balinese *bales*, other than the thick thatched roofs, are the teak posts that support them. Called *sasakas*, these posts are simply beautiful, squared off below, they rise through a *paduraksa*, a carved design that transforms the post from four to eight-sided above. The dimensions of the posts are determined by a series of spans taken off the hand, which, added together, become the *rahi*, the basic unit of measurement used to carpenter the posts. Below the *paduraksa*, the posts are one *rahi* to a side. Because this is a variable, rather than a standard measurement, Balinese carpenters traditionally had to hew the posts to measure. The length of the posts, a multiple of the *rahi* and a single finger *urip*, like the width, are standard throughout the compound, and contribute to the harmony of the whole. Though the height of my posts occasioned giggles all around, it felt right to me, and I stood looking up at the tape measure extended to 264 centimeters for a long time, satisfied.

It was while we were taping the *depa agung* that I stepped in the chicken shit. I reached as high as I could with my left arm, and rose up onto the toes of my right foot, stretching, then let myself down once the measurement was taken, barefoot into a little pile of chicken shit. I felt mocked, but not by my hosts. They were sorry, and Ketut's wife led limping me back to the *kelod* corner of the compound, where she poured a bucket of water over my foot. Too many chickens, was all she said.

After that, my passion for a house fitting flagged. We talked. Young Wayan explained that the gate opening into the compound was measured from elbow to elbow when, hands on hips, the elbows were held out, arms akimbo. The width of the doors inside the compound was taken off the head, like a hat size, and my fat head elicited a round of soft chuckles: it would be easy to get the furniture in and out, anyway. Wayan sketched a compound of four *bales*, something appropriate for a small family. He shaded the grounds around the pavilions with quick pencil strokes, Swastika, he said, indicating the shape of the darkened ground. Clockwise-turning, a Hindu swastika, like a clock face with the hours ticking forward.

After a traditional Balinese compound is built, a priest is called in and through a series of ceremonies the buildings are brought to life. The trees and bamboo, the very grasses used for thatch, everything that was sacrificed in the construction of the *bales*, is reincarnated into new life. Thereafter, the pavilions are thought of as alive and treated with respect. On ceremonial occasions, they may even be dressed, like people. The roof corresponds to the head, the posts to the body, and the foundation to the feet. Alive. In the west, I think, we are far more likely to characterize architecture as dead than living, though to say dead testifies, perhaps, to an unacknowledged desire to inhabit a world that at least feels alive.

Before we left, Young Wayan cautioned me that what we'd done was but a primer, that *asta kosala kosali* was far more complex than what we'd been able to cover. But I already knew that: everything in Bali is more complicated than you'd think, just looking. I thanked them, thanked them all, and bowed my head deeply over my tented hands when I said goodbye to Old Wayan, who'd been the one best able to animate our discussion, to make me feel the house in my body.

::

On the drive back to Ubud, Made asked about my house back home, and I found that in Balinese terms there was little to say of it. A three-bedroom stucco bungalow, built about 1920. How the sun tracks in winter. The view over the graveyard to blue hills. A house not defined so much by what it is as by what's in it. That speaks, has meaning, but in an idiosyncratic way.

Ahead, we saw two horsemen rounding a curve. Westerners. Somehow they had sparked a commotion, and just as we began to swing left, following the narrow paved track, a cow jumped out of a raised field, over a wide drainage ditch, smack onto the pavement in front of us. She was that cow jumping over the moon in the illustrated *Mother Goose*, hooves high fore and aft, head thrown back. When she landed it was as if on ice, her legs churning on the slippery pavement; but she regained her balance and charged on down, across the road and into a field, running, her tether streaming behind her. I wouldn't have thought that jump possible—how what's credible can suddenly expand! We laughed. What looked like an accident, a disaster for someone, resolved into a great joke. And that calf, peering out of the long grass of the upper field after its mother, must have been wondering what that jump was all about!

When I arrived back at Nirvana, Nyoman was drinking Bali coffee, and he poured me a cup, and I told him all about my house fitting. He sympathized that the architect and his family had found me big, comically big, because, as he said, he was big, too. But I think he found me a little cracked on the subject of *gagulaks*. I asked him if the architects had notched *gagulaks* for him when he'd had the villa built out in the rice fields, saying I'd like to see them. They had. But I didn't keep them, he said. Why would I? I still have my body, and he made a sweeping motion with his free hand. My measure is right here!

::

The next time I saw Made he asked me if I'd be interested in visiting a couple of house compounds in Batuan. Old style, totally original, he said. Very cheap to see, almost free. I was interested, but I thought the old ways must be passing more quickly than I'd realized if there was now a business in showing them. House museums! Could dioramas be far behind? Still, Let's go, was all I said.

But the first place was under renovation, perhaps the proceeds from visitors paying for a renewal that made the place less traditional every day—an irony familiar to travelers everywhere, their arrival hastening the end of the very thing they've come to see. Workers in shades were rebuilding the low interior walls that separated the family temple, with its ancestor shrines, from the rest of the compound. Yards of smooth cement had been poured in. Pre-cast decorative elements and terra cotta brick. Everything ruler straight and crisp. The harmonies of *asta kosala kosali*, the human proportions, were lost to sight. And the soft edges of use, of touch, had been obliterated where the work was new and made to look shabby in what was still old. The graying man who showed us around—and he looked a little out of place against the new walls, too— was visibly pleased with what money had wrought. He hadn't bought a refrigerator for the cookhouse, after all; his first thought had been to get right with the gods. That old man, so small, his wrinkled body had folded up as if made ready to be put away. He took my hand in his as I was leaving, smiling, something in him warm and expansive, still alive to the momentary connection of a chance meeting.

The ground of the second compound had been paved with rounded river stones. Although the shape of the earth had been smoothed, some of the original contours of the site were still visible. A few beds for bushes and flowers had been created with a curb of raised stones, but they were not so many. A little dirt showed in the pigs' corner. Here and there a small palm or fig created a patch of welcome shade. Four ducks huddled together near the well.

Entering, we had passed through a roofed gate, and by a screening wall, the *aling-aling*, built just inside. Although the gate was massively built, I'd felt the pinch of a small man's arms-akimbo passing through, and a sudden sense of opening in stepping around the stone screening wall: here, you entered, not grandly, but definitely. Inside, it felt a protected world, a walled garden. The effect was not only visual; there were small shrine boxes on each side of the gate, where the potency of the gate's protection is renewed daily with offerings, and the *aling-aling* was not just there to visually screen the compound from the street, but also to keep evil out, which traditional Balinese believe only travels in a straight line.

The center of a Balinese compound is left open, an interior courtyard that all the *bales* face. In a modest compound like this one, none of the *bales* are big enough to suggest the word "house." They seem more like outbuildings without the big house, or free standing rooms, each with its own raised foundation and thatched roof. Except for the north building, which is enclosed, about half of what the pavilions have under roof is covered porch. Public and private space are zoned very differently here than in the west. Our urban model is domestic and private inside, public space immediately outside, sidewalks and the street. Our suburban model, a house in a green, is domestic and private inside, semi-private outside. In a Balinese compound, the whole lot is private and domestic, walled, but there is very little personal privacy, very little private space behind walls. It's an arrangement that fosters a sense of family, while discouraging self-regard. Solidarity over isolation.

Somehow the freestanding *bales*, each separate, but all of them in a family way featuring teak posts, thatched roofs, and mud walls, possess a kind of casual clarity, nothing crowded, nothing too close or closed, everything distinct. Oriented *kaja* and *kelod*, east and west, up and down, each *bale* with its specified uses. It's an order achieved, but not taken for granted. Not only is the entry to the compound protected from malign influence by the gate and the screening wall, but the pattern that the river stones take, laid out on the ground, describes a rough Hindu swastika; even birds of the air would be able to see that the place is protected.

Made whispered to me, This place is very interesting, and again I realized that this is a passing world, which modern Bali has begun to forget. The quiet authority of the compound, everything built according to an articulated plan, no reaching, no showiness, would soon count as a rarity. The measure of the particular man who first lived here, who stood still while the carpenters notched the strips of bamboo off his body according to the old formula's of *asta kosala kosali*, his measure seemed more symbolic than crucial to the particular proportions of the place. Any man—or woman—would do about as well. What matters most is the gesture to the human body, an honoring, and an acknowledgment that we are made flesh, that our living takes place in a human world, our life in the larger life of that place.

We walked through, visitors in a passing world. In one corner the ancestor shrines, dressed, and at the other end, the rail fence of the sty. Everything swept and quiet. Before we left, an old woman stepped down out of a *bale* to greet us. The years had had their way with her. Dressed only in a sarong pulled tight around her waist, she might have been one of the girls painted by Walter Spies or William Gerard Hofker in the '30s and '40s, when from the west Bali had an Edenic look. Then, the traditional ways were less remembered than just lived. That girl had weathered down to this, friendliness a matter of fact, warm eyes, a gap-toothed smile. We touched hands. Made made the polite inquiries and she laughed, pointing around the compound with the small staff in her left hand. Looking at her, I thought we all die in a past world, and that this is as it should be, and acceptable.

::

A journey ends. But before I left the island I wanted to see that girl again, my favorite condong, in the legong dance of the youth troop in Peliatan. Not, maybe, the most technically proficient condong around Ubud, and not the most elegant, either; she nevertheless danced with incomparable authority. She was visited by the dance, and the dance possessed her so completely that her body seemed to disappear within the flashing body of the dance itself. A world all electric. A dance-lit room.

The free transport proved an old van; only four of us boarded in central Ubud for the short trip to Peliatan. Two old guys from Osaka chattered in the back, to each other, and to a young woman from Kyoto who sat across the aisle from me. After the introductions, I kept to myself, sank into the melancholy of the half-illuminated night scenes flitting by beyond the glass. I saw the eyes of the driver in the rearview mirror, his attention taken up by the Japanese. Perhaps the girl from Kyoto appealed to him, reserved, but willing to humor the old men. Or perhaps it was the old men themselves, their high spirits rendered harmless by age.

When the van stopped I was the first one out, walking the long alley to the dance hall alone in the dark. I wanted that chair in front, but I liked the dark alley, too, and preferred it alone. The moon's radiant progress. The slow rain of all those southern stars going west.

I got the chair, but the condong who danced that night was not my girl, but another girl, beautiful and elegant, the better technician, no doubt the better dancer. But she did not combust. It did not feel, for the space of a dance, that where she stood the earth circled round.

I felt chagrinned, a little silly. And I sat quietly in my chair the rest of the evening. The last dance of the night was topeng, the masked old man. He tottered out onto the stage, as if surprised to find himself there, lit up and on display. Although he still wore the opulent clothes of a court gentleman, the old man seemed bewildered by them, in danger of tripping himself up. And when he tried to dance, he stumbled. His hair, formerly black and neat, now sprouted from his head white, long, and disheveled. A great white mustache hung from his upper lip. Worse, he searched his flesh like a man plagued by nits and fleas.

I sat in the small crowd, silent; we were all silent, lost in a great mirror.

This old man, he came right up to the stage edge, in front of the footlights, gesturing, reaching out a palsied hand to the Japanese girl from the van. He beckoned, she cringed. He begged, she relented. She stood up and put her hand in his, and the old man beamed, for a second, and then he dropped her hand, stumbling back, resuming not the dance but his failure to dance. The girl sat down, embarrassed, while the old man climbed the stairs to his exit.

::

The Southern Cross hung low in the alley as I walked back to the van. When I arrived, the driver was already there, and feeling talkative. He complained about the heat, and his face did glisten, wet. A breeze, cool and sweet, touched me lightly, moving on. I was dancing, the driver said, hot. The lights and the costume, very hot. Which dance, I asked, what part? The old man, he said shyly, perhaps a little mischievously, and we laughed together as the Japanese walked up. When I told her, the girl from Kyoto wouldn't believe it. Not really so old, the driver said. Not yet.

(2005)

COLORS

::

Mean, but amusing, I've always thought, the disappointed critic who wrote of Hugo von Hoffmannsthal that he would have been a great poet if he'd died at twenty-five. Maybe so. I didn't object to the dismissive note struck by the wit when I first encountered it, even though at the time Hoffmannsthal meant a great deal to me. I had read the poetry, even the librettos, with interest, but for me it was Hoffmannsthal's prose that mattered, especially his "Colours," a traveler's tale.

Then, strangely enough, for many years I remembered the reviewer's witticism without remembering the story recounted in "Colours." Until my old friend Tom brought it up—and hadn't I, once upon a time, been the one who'd recommended Hoffmannsthal to him? We were discussing an essay I had written about Cambodia, which opened with a description of a statue of a Khmer goddess, a passage that, Tom said, reminded him of "Colours." And I saw that it was so. I saw in "Colours" the model of all my far flung museum-going. It felt odd, thinking Hoffmannsthal in "Colours" had made me.

Hoffmannsthal's traveler—a business traveler!—has returned home to Europe after what seems to have been years abroad, in South America, in Asia. He's finding being back more difficult than being there, in that the felt reality of things slips away from him from time to time now that he has returned home. Just anything might suddenly feel "so utterly not real," and "To look at them caused me an almost imperceptible nausea: it was like a momentary floating above the abyss, the eternal void." Nothing in his travels had ever affected him in this way, suspended him over absence, his familiar radically estranged. And American reality has failed me too, sometimes, and in just this way, after long sojourns abroad, the nausea only ebbing away when the agreed-on world jelled again around me. Although Hoffmannsthal's traveler's account suggests there is a role for the corrosive effect of one consensual reality on another, he insists his malady is specifically European, because it only besets him coming home, never going. And I, too, have often felt traveling that the lands I journeyed through were just—somehow—more real. Hoffmannsthal's traveler concludes that it's the way westerners covet money that makes the difference, that "they forgot life itself in favor of that which should be nothing but a means toward life and should be nothing but a tool." And the things themselves that such a compromised culture throws up slide into the unreal. Hoffmannsthal's business traveler feels he is implicated in all this, and the revulsion turns inward.

What restores the traveler at the last hour—more than restores him—is a chance visit to an art exhibit featuring the work of Vincent van Gogh. The year of the story is 1901, and Hoffmannsthal's traveler has never heard of the painter. Still, in the paints, in their colors, "the innermost life of objects" broke through:

> the Being of each tree, each strip of yellow or greenish
> field, each fence, each gorge cut into the stony hill,

> the Being of the pewter jug, the earthen bowl, the table, the clumsy armchair—lifted itself toward me as though newly born from the frightful chaos of Non-living, from the abyss of Non-Being, so that I felt—nay, so that I knew—how each of these objects, these creatures, was born from a terrible doubting of the world and how with its existence it now covered over forever the dreadful chasm of yawning nothingness!

Suddenly, a world ecstatically present, a surfeit of the real. Hoffmannsthal's traveler presumes this radiant world is always there, and we would know it, but for the "inner constant sleep" that cloaks it from us.

I'm afraid my characterization of Hoffmannsthal's "Colours" verges on caricature. Hoffmannsthal's art is subtle, beginning with his choice of the unsophisticated business traveler as his narrator, but I want to write large here, to make the structure show. The going, the return to what begins to feel an unreal place, and out of extreme distress an extreme response to art encountered by chance, in which art possesses, then heals you.

For a moment, rereading "Colours," it seemed to me that Hoffmannsthal had laid down the pattern, and that my experience had done no more than conform to it. Feeling ghostly, written, I turned to the fly leaf and read the date I had bought the Hoffmannsthal: Spring 1974, two years *after* the first of the experiences I'd been thinking about, and the causal explanation at first suggested by my rereading of "Colours" suddenly seemed too neat.

::

KEVIN ODERMAN

Prado : Black

July 1972

That year I went traveling, for the first time, really, on the three thousand dollars my father had given me when I graduated from college. The gift was money enough then to buy a tired Volkswagen bug and drive around Europe for months. In many ways, I was traveling under the influence of Nikos Kazantzakis, who had launched me into the world. His *Report to Greco* had been the very book. So, in Spain, I wanted especially to see the El Grecos that had meant so much to Kazantzakis.

That's all true, but way too matter of fact. I was shattered that year, somewhere near the middle of a prolonged spiritual—or if you prefer psychological—crisis. I hadn't slept normally for many months, and a good part of my bed time was spent failing to master my writhing guts. And yet I was never without a caustic pot of tea at my elbow, cranking up the mental wattage as I turned to the next page of whatever book I was reading. I hardly ate, a few dates or dried Greek figs. I weighed twenty pounds less than I had in eighth grade. I dreamed of thinking my way through the problems that haunted me. And then I realized, bone deep, that that was not going to happen.

I called the University of Toronto, where I had accepted a fellowship for the following year, and told them I wouldn't be attending. I didn't have an alternate plan, and in the absence of any plan I should have backed out of the wedding set for June, too, but I didn't. I didn't then realize that the crueler thing was to marry. That girl, who I must now call my first wife, we were traveling together in the VW bug, or side by side. We plunged through the days. The world that swam into sight repelled or enchanted me, I was gasping. And I had started to write, which meant I was listening intently to the words in my head, so intently that though I was present in body I was often absent as a companion. "Hello? Anybody home?" A hand like a windshield wiper waved back and forth in front of my face.

I had written before, in high school, notebooks of poetry, but in college I'd set that aside to study hard. Then, it's a coincidence odd and suggestive, on the very night I married I was startled out of bed by an insistent voice in my ear: "Their breathing out is our breathing in." I got up and wrote the poem down, embers from the fire in the hearth of that little cabin on Puget Sound falling quietly through the grate, slowly burning down to ash. "Their dark harkenings are our darker intimations." These years on, I quote the lines from memory; whatever else can be said of them, they arrived with authority. And what an image to begin! The very first line an image of inspiration itself, to receive the breath. But it's not an image altogether pleasant, this inspiration, somewhere between mouth-to-mouth resuscitation and a suffocating kiss. I didn't wonder whose breath I was breathing in, I knew. Dead poets all: Georg Trakl, Rainer Maria Rilke, grand and mad Friedrich Hölderlin.

In Spain I gravitated to Toledo, El Greco's town, which I had read about not only in Kazantzakis but also in Rilke's impassioned prose. An old town on a hill in a loop of the Río Tajo, so intensely present I felt that at any moment it might suddenly combust in the implacable sun. El Greco's *The Burial of Count Orgaz*. His aristocrats and saints, large eyes upturned and wet with yearning. Everyone dressed in one color, it seemed, or two, robes green or red or orange or brown, the aristocrats in black with a white ruff. The aristocrats self-contained, the saints one and all about to split their carapace. Yearning for transcendence. To finish up and be gone. I think I wanted that, too.

In Madrid, our first visit to the Prado began and ended in the El Greco rooms. We just left, the rest of the museum unvisited, El Greco more than enough for me. She indulged me too much, that girl at my side, a waif, the innocent face of the '60s and the long brown hair, but she was worried or should have been. We went back to the Prado again, another day, to the El Greco rooms, and walked out a second time. On the third visit I thought I'd look around, stroll away from what I imagined had called me there. That's how it is: most of the time traveling we don't know what we're in for. In many ways I was green, ignorant as the young are ignorant, and arrogant about the few things I did know. Perhaps I had never even heard of the black Goyas, that's possible, and I walked into them like a man missing a stair, falling into glossy blackness. No transcendence there, just this world, and all of us ineluctably in it. Two old men eating, their final lust for just anything to stuff their faces, their hunger obscene. Almost as disturbing as *Saturn*, wild eyed, gnawing on his own son. This world as nightmare. The appalling storytelling in *Goat*, the audience in what feels surely to be an evil trance. I was not repelled, walking through those rooms, but rapt. Blatant and us, Goya's *Fight with Cudgels*. And perhaps because the war was on in Vietnam, the firing squad in *The Executions: The Third of May*, spoke urgently, shouted *No*, as did *The Colossus*, with its spectral giant striding confidently through an embattled landscape.

Right there, falling headlong into the black vision of *The Colossus*, I whispered the opening of Trakl's last poem, "Grodek," a poem named for the town where in 1914 the Great War had ended for him. There, in charge of an ill-equipped field hospital housed in a small barn, he'd overseen the terrible suffering of ninety wounded soldiers, unable to relieve their agonies. One soldier, in extremity, shot himself in the head, blowing his brains and chips of his skull against the wall of the barn. Trakl, unhinged himself, reeled outside, only to be met there by the bodies of executed partisans hanging in the encircling trees. He broke, quickly spiraling down to a young poet's suicide in the psychiatric ward of a hospital in Cracow:

> At nightfall the autumn woods cry out
> With deadly weapons and the golden plains,
> The deep blue lakes, above which more darkly
> Rolls the sun; the night embraces
> Dying warriors, the wild lament
> Of their broken mouths.
> But quietly there in the pastureland
> Red clouds in which an angry god resides,
> The shed blood gathers, lunar coolness.
> All roads lead to blackest carrion.

::

Lahore Museum : Black

September 1996

I had been on my way to Lahore for months, traveling in Greece and Turkey with a woman who had been working in Germany for a year. We had resumed a life together, rendezvoused in Berlin, then flown on to Athens, where we boarded a ferry south and then another east, together watching the sea birds plunge in the wake. Walking a stone track on Patmos—or was it Symi?—telling her stories, I tried to explain how after a divorce a few years earlier I had fled to Greece, and ferried south through the Cyclades and on to Crete, then on again, all the way to Alexandria.

And how in my grief I had been overtaken by a bizarre fascination with the cow-eared goddess, Hathor. Once, I told my companion, I had even shimmied up a column at a temple on the Nile dedicated to Hathor, at Dendera, and kissed that goddess on the mouth. Crazy, I meant, silly and not like me at all: what a mess I'd been. The wind swirled around us, and my green-eyed friend peered at me oddly through her loose, dark curls. She was jealous. Of Hathor. She couldn't get that kiss out of her head and kept bringing it up long after my surprise had turned to deep dismay. "You can't be jealous of a goddess," I cried out at last, but she could be, she was. And after that she was jealous of pretty much everything and everybody else.

A door closed. I traveled on to Lahore alone. Golden Lahore, it had been, but just dusty by the time I got there. Still, there were apparitions in the dust. Dust devils twirling in a vacant lot and the urgent voice of *qawwali*, sweet mulberries hanging from a tree and the ammoniac stains of pissed-on walls. The living smoldered, ashy, then leapt up like flame. And my own voice, calling, exhorting, "This is poetry," in the high-ceilinged classrooms of Punjab University, "listen."

Outside, the "gents" in their white *shalwar kamis*, and the "ladies," in *shalwar kamis*, too, but theirs dipped in intense blues or yellows or purples, like painted birds, clustered together or strolling in twos and threes in front of the red walls of the English building. At the end of the drive, the traffic on the Mall, and across that the National College of Art and the Lahore Museum. Of course, I crossed that street, entered the galleries in the museum and turned left, walked to the end, and stopped, there where the serenity of the black Gandharan Buddhas and bodhisattvas stilled everything. Stilled my heart. A great gallery of them, suave and black, as if carved out of the stuff of night itself, as if nothingness itself found expression in them. Yet their expression is replete: nothing more is wanted, nothing more could be wanted.

Desire, even the desire to gaze and be lost in those faces, was checked in that cool room. A perfect black hand gesturing, "Yes, yes. Everything just so."

I remember I walked down the aisle to those statues light with expectation. Not once, but many times. By the two big, antique carpets displayed flat and a rack of small ones, hanging. I could look at them, piece together their intricate designs, before I got to the black statues. About leaving, about re-crossing the perilous Mall, I don't remember a thing. Of course the tall trees loomed over the entry to the university just as before, alive with parrots often, maybe a hoopoe poking around on the lawn. But it seems, at least now in memory, that the wild chatterings and dark mutterings of Pakistan were extinguished by where I had been.

::

Bhaktapur Art Gallery : Gold

May 1997

I remember I couldn't sleep through the night in Kathmandu, that sometime late I'd find myself awake, the room lit a little by moonlight falling through the shutters. Just the walls, the standard pallor of whitewash gone slightly yellow. The standing walls, not ominous, barely there, at the minims of being. I remember sitting on the edge of my bed, my feet flat on the cool tiles, just for the feel of them on the soles of my feet, for contact. Standing, peering out between the slats of the shutters down an empty alley, to a street where perhaps someone would pass, a street that would be lively again if tomorrow ever got here. Back in bed, I remember thinking about the past, faces rising out of the murk, one framed in hair in dark curls; someone sad and bold, a very painted smile; someone gliding over like a bird on still wings, her upturned face looking away. There's nothing like traveling alone to call the past up close. In isolation, the mind teems with the absent, the gone, and the long gone.

And as if the isolation of a year teaching in Lahore was not enough, I isolated myself further at every chance. The glittering murals at Wat Phra Kaeo, in Bangkok, where gravity was abridged, and it seemed possible to fly; Bangkok, where at midnight, standing in the humming darkness at a filthy pay phone, I made a call to say goodbye. Another face for a sleepless night. Or a rail journey into the hill country in Sri Lanka, traveling first class in the saloon car, coupled at the front of the train, pushed up and around, through forests and tea plantations. Kandy, a single stroll around the lake, the fishman swimming on a roof beam in The Temple of the Tooth, looking blistered and black around the eyes, but he seemed to be me, however unlikely. Then a small silver plane dropping through thin air, the Himalayas close and terribly bright in my window, white pennants of cloud pulled out of the peaks as if by sleight of hand. Down, down into the darkening valley, Kathmandu. Trips not planned but just taken. In retrospect, I think I took those trips to be yet more alone than I found myself in Lahore, that isolation always figured large in my destinations, that it promised a pruning. I don't remember what I told myself then.

In Kathmandu, insomnia took over my nights. The days seemed to elongate, the deep seriousness of the Buddhist and Hindu sites oddly framed by the circus of western travelers and the locals there to fleece them. Outside of costume parties, I'd never seen such a colorful band of pretenders. The evening walk to dinner through half-lit streets proved an exercise in saying *no* to the pimps and dealers who swarmed in the shadows. Then the long nights. Exhaustion wore me away.

I began to make excursions out of Kathmandu. I took my insomnia up to the lip of the valley, to Nagarkot, and got up before dawn to walk the ridge and gaze at the big mountains as they lit up at sunrise. I bowed my head at the great stupas; I walked down through the compound of Pashupatinath on the banks of the holy Bagmati, considered the twists of smoke rising up there from the burning ghats. I disappeared into the beauty of the architecture in old Kathmandu, in old Patan, my mind suffused with the soft red brick and the intricately carved, bleached wood out of which that world is made.

Another day I hired a car to drive me to the far end of Kathmandu valley, to visit the capital of the third of the valley's medieval kingdoms, Bhaktapur. Extreme light and shadow. The whole of Durbar Square might have been hallucination, so little did it correspond to the "real world" of modern America. And almost deserted. I was there, vagrant, a pilgrim. Off the square, I wandered through arcades where sheaves were being threshed by people who didn't seem to see me, by the open doors of shops where the only sound was the rough whir of a potter's wheel. In the square the temple gods had been freshly smeared with flowers, with ochre, the bright pigments glowing against walls blackened by the soot of butter lamps. A warning, "For Hinduse Only." Just past a golden gate I saw a small sign, "Art Gallery," and I turned in, a museum. The guards couldn't be bothered to follow me through the few high rooms. I walked on alone, the sound of my footsteps the only proof I was there. On a table set in full sun—in front of a window or was it an open door?—a god and a goddess faced each other in a passionate embrace, each of them surrounded by a whirl of arms, like a peacock's fan, hands wrapped around knives, weapons, their bird heads face to face, tongues out, screeching, it seemed, screaming, the light bounding from their bronze bodies like flames. On the table, in my head. Not killing each other, but sex, the terrible combat of their opposite natures joining together. I was alone, I stepped close and reached my hand under them, feeling for the truth; they were already joined. Their coupling was understood, I knew, as an achieved unity, as wholeness. But not serene, no. I felt buffeted about the head as if by an eagle's great wings.

::

Sackler : Color

August 1998

I had seen wadded fragments of central Asian ikat in the Afgan market in Lahore in 1997, but I hadn't known how to see them. I hadn't had a good look. On a couple of occasions I had rummaged through drawers of rumpled textiles in a passageway between a showroom and a storage room, in a carpet shop run by ethnic Uzbeks—camel trappings, yurt decorations, suzanis and Lakai embroideries, dirty chapan robes. A real hodgepodge. I remember there were some splashy, colorful scraps; I think now they probably were pure silk or adras ikat. Perhaps they reminded me too much of the hippie tie-dyes of the '60s; probably they looked too bright to live with the old things I was chasing in Lahore. Perhaps it was the level of dirt, dust rising up in clouds under a single electric bulb, grime and stains on almost everything. The ikats didn't speak to me. The prospects looked more promising in the big room stacked with carpets and kilims, Balouch and Uzbek bags, but now I wish I had stayed to look until I'd learned to see the ikats.

CANNOT STAY

In the summer of 1998, Delta B. and I were new, traveling together perhaps for the first time. In D.C., we rocketed around town, showing each other favorite things. My favorite museum was the Sackler, underground on the Mall, near the Smithsonian headquarters; Delta favored the Freer, the green and gold Peacock Room and the Whistlers.

We were sharing enthusiasms, hoping, I suppose, to create shared enthusiasms. At the Sackler, I wanted Delta to love the little Khmer goddess I'd been carrying on with for years, the very Khmer goddess that would subsequently take me to Cambodia, the one I would write about in a way that would remind my friend Tom of Hoffmannsthal's "Colours," which led me to consider what museumgoing might be all about, and here I am, writing again.

At the goddess, I think, Delta sniffed (I am slow to learn). But it must be confessed, my own affections for the little Khmer statue proved fickle that day, that day when I finally saw the ikats. The poster outside announcing the show read, I know, "Ikat: Splendid Silks of Central Asia from the Guido Goldman Collection." I must have seen it. But, in memory, it seems we simply plunged into color. The mustard taste of yellow, pomegranate red. Bathing in blue. Bound by a green cord. The deep-shade feel of indigo. The plump sound of aubergine. Vermillion. Black and white, too. Not one color as quiet as a color alone; every one of them loving its neighbors. An orgy.

The intricate repeating designs seemed devised foremost to make the color stronger, to make it overwhelming. From the first enormous wall-hanging, the beauty, the color, was too much. We didn't leave, but what we saw bled, synesthesia. You could hear the colors, taste them. No, we didn't leave. Sixty-six ikats coming and going. They were hanging everywhere, every one of them too much. Our experience dyed in color.

I bought the catalog on the way out and subsequently read all about the ikats. There's a lot to know, as it turns out, and it's interesting, but nothing in the catalog could make the experience of just looking at the ikats more intense, and I suppose the danger in all such knowing is that a scrim of words might come to stand between art and experience, subduing naïve experience. I suppose I was lucky to see the ikats first.

The great era of ikat production in central Asia was short lived, starting early in the nineteenth century and finished by the fourth quarter when chemical dyes were introduced. The weavings are associated with the route of the old Silk Road, with Bukhara and Samarkand and the Ferghana Valley, in contemporary Uzbekistan and Tajikistan. Large hangings, like the ones that predominate in the Guido Goldman Collection, were meant to suggest a flowering garden, to make of mud-plastered walls a reminder of the walled gardens of paradise.

Although robes tailored from silk and silk velvet ikats no doubt accounted for most of ikat production in central Asia, the exhibit at the Sackler included only a few examples. These coats are so incandescent, so outward turning, that I was astonished to read that to make a show both men and women sometimes wore them as many as ten deep, robe over radiant robe. I have tried to imagine getting dressed up like that, putting them on, each one as brilliant as the one before, the body slowly losing its human shape to a bud of thickening color. Would the flesh seem to darken or feel as if it was about to break open in gorgeous bloom?

::

The Textile Museum : Color

January 2003

Up into the blue mountains and down again, the road scrolling out in front of our turning wheels and then a world flattening and the slow glide into traffic, D.C. again, not seen so much as felt in the quickening pulse of things. Even in the District the low buildings hide the enormous city. We had checked into a hotel near Dupont Circle before we finally registered we were there. What seemed a rare astrological conjunction had called us to town for a weekend in the museums. Saturday night they would close the doors on the Pierre Bonnard exhibit at The Phillips Collection, and we wanted to get there before that happened; then Sunday, an Edouard Vuillard exhibit would open at the National Gallery of Art. Delta B.'s every step looked like dance. How lucky I felt when we stood side by side in front of Bonnard's *Women with Dog* or when we leaned our heads together over the two girls in the mysterious *Reflecting on the Day*. Extravagant color, the world resolved in color. And then the Vuillards, the women in figured dresses half sunk in the figure of the wallpaper, in the cut flowers, in *The Dressing Table*, color too but somber, perhaps a little more in accord with my inner weather. And how we went back and back to see again the so-lovely *Seamstress with Scraps*, the humble *Mantlepiece*. Bonnard and Vuillard were friends, old friends when they drifted apart to their own corners of France to paint and to die. Ghosts now, here they were crossing each other's paths in another century, in another country. They had rallied together as young men, with other like-minded painters, styling themselves the *Nabis*—prophets—a name unlikely for artists so enamored of a world domestic and decorative. As a young man, I wouldn't have esteemed these artists' ability to find the everyday world so thick with beauty. Everydayness wasn't what I'd wanted, not at all. Perhaps I wasn't so interested in beauty, either. I wanted to be split open, like firewood opened by an axe. Riven. Ready for a match.

Now, common happiness seems a desirable if not a final good. That weekend in the city gave us a glowing respite from winter. We met again our young friend Jessie, all sound and earnest promise, went out for Thai and then the three of us sitting in our rumpled coats with popcorn in a theater, *The Hours* flickering away on the screen. Breakfast at Teaism, smoked salmon in the scrambled eggs and a pot of sweet and milky Assam, the winter light standing white in the window. Everything shot through with common joy. The world as praised by Bonnard and Vuillard.

That weekend, as we do, Delta and I went walking. The Textile Museum was in range. The city guide said Mamluk rugs were on, Egyptian and very old, late fifteenth and early sixteenth century. Somewhere in the years I had come to love old textiles, especially nomadic things. The way the makers of tribal rugs started with nothing but sheep and what they knew of dyestuffs, the way the rugs expressed both imagination and tradition. And I had an interest in Egypt, too, first fired by reading Lawrence Durrell's *Quartet*, which had led to an overnight ferry from Kazantzakis' hometown of Iraklion on Crete to Alexandria, then a bus through the desert to Cairo, and a train on to Luxor, not least because of Rilke's clairvoyant essay on the temple at nearby Karnak. I'd wanted to see. The Valley of the Kings, thinking about the poet H.D. and her lover Bryher, in 1922, going out to watch Howard Carter empty the tomb of that boy Tutankhamen. Then Aswan, and back down the Nile to Dendera, where I'd kissed the goddess Hathor. All this years before. City guide in hand, wondering how to pronounce Mamluk, Egypt swirled up around me once again.

At the Textile Museum we turned right from the entry down the hall to the Mamluk rugs. I wasn't prepared, that's all. Perhaps I couldn't have been. Mamluk rugs have no known precedent and had no subsequent influence, but seem to stand outside carpet-weaving traditions. Perhaps that disconnection contributes to how they feel, otherworldly. Outside the known world. The inspired geometry of their design, yes, but also an unusual, restricted palette; most of the rugs are red, blue, and green. But somehow the colors are so harmonious it seems that they must all be variations of a single color, that the radiating astral medallions and geometric frames might at any moment disappear in one beauty. And they did. Again and again the sheen, the amazing luster of the wool itself, rose up a single field of ravishing blue light and obliterated all figure.

::

In Hoffmannsthal's story "Colours," after the business traveler has visited the gallery, seen the van Goghs, he "hailed a carriage" and drove directly to a business meeting he had been dreading, not surprisingly given his persistent feeling of "floating above the abyss." There, in an inspired state, he did better for his company than the "most optimistic hopes" of his board of directors.

On reflection, I find this turn of events a bit puzzling. Doesn't the traveler's success in the world of business suggest a restoration of consensual, business values, a return to the world of valuing experience according to monetary standards? Perhaps Hoffmannsthal imagined that to recognize the traveler's transformed state most western readers would need it to register in the world of money. Perhaps Hoffmannsthal just thought that such experiences in fact make one better able to function in consensual reality, and maybe that's so. His main interests are certainly elsewhere, in the "inner wordless certainties" that his traveler takes from the experience, "like a swelling in [his] breast, an abundance, a strange, exalted, enchanting presence."

I know the museumgoing experiences I've described here never proved a financial boon for me, at least never in so direct a way as Hoffmannsthal imagines for his narrator in "Colours." But then, I'm not a business traveler; I've never sat down in a boardroom to make a deal.

It occurs to me that it's my old friend Tom who has become a business traveler, though it's his own business, a concern he created to avoid the busyness of working for someone else, and he doesn't deal in things. Still, he's made over fifty extended trips abroad, and I know wherever he goes he visits the local museums, that his own sense of reality is buttressed by seeing art. He's the big redhead, the thoughtful guy looking over your shoulder, at ease, ready to be impressed.

Much has been written about the difficulties of seeing art in museums, about how the presentation tends to overwhelm the work itself, and I think that's so. Still, most of the art we need to see is in museums, and it's in traveling that we get to see it. And there are advantages in this, because traveling we tend to be unsettled, perhaps readier to see than we would be at home, and "Readiness is all."

Another advantage of museum-going is that what we see is not for sale. We won't be buying it. We must find another way to value it or we won't be valuing it at all. Shoppers feel uneasy, can be heard muttering dollar values, and perhaps spend more time in the gift shop than in the museum proper, but their uneasiness speaks opportunity. Sleepers might be shaken awake, the broken might find their distresses eased. It happens all the time, if perhaps not as neatly as Hoffmannsthal's "Colours" suggests. "Colours" is a work of art itself, after all, and for me, healing. Hoffmannsthal's narrator never suggests that van Gogh's paintings are realistic, instead he insists that they were "born from a terrible doubting of the world" and that they in some mysterious way "answer the spasms of his own most dreadful doubt."

When I think about it in light of my own museumgoing, "Colours" seems compromised by the strictures of narrative, by its being a story, perhaps. One thing coming first and leading to another. It seems to me more likely that the elements of the story form a loose net, that a tug anywhere on it makes the net move, and maybe not all of it. Often we go traveling not because we've been sent on business but because life at home has come to seem a deep sleep or because we feel broken. Perfect well-being is not much of an instigation. Art can heal us but also unsettle us, travel too. And surprise can take us at home or abroad, whenever we find ourselves outside of our expectations. I'm not saying I object to Hoffmannsthal's narrative art, that "Colours" is a story. It works, it makes visible, and memorable, experiences I had both before and after I read it. I don't see any advantage in wanting it to be something it's not.

Hoffmannsthal, in "Colours," suggests that the traveler's kind of rapt response to art arises out of unknowing, that it is about as far from the connoisseur's knowing response as you can get. And in reviewing my own experiences in museums, I have found my most ecstatic moments have always been attended by surprise. Don't think this means I don't value knowledge, a learned response to art. But between the traveler's kind of knowing and the connoisseur's there is a gap, and I think it's good to remember that while you can go from unknowing to knowing, you can't go back. So I think it's best to look first, to avoid the guidebooks, the docents, the audio tours, even the labels as long as you can, to prefer the thing to the language it's wrapped in. There will be time enough for studying later.

Even before I read Hoffmannsthal I was aware of the dangers, from a line in Rilke's *Sonnets to Orpheus*. As it turns out, I've misquoted it for years, saying "like the blue of a flower whose name I don't know." I thought I understood, how the color of a flower could be usurped by its name—blue bell or cornflower—how not knowing the name we look closer. Colors again. But checking the quotation I was surprised to discover that Rilke's sonnet actually reads, "But you now, you whom I knew like a flower whose name/ I don't know..." Not a color, but a girl, Wera Ouckama Knoop, for whom the *Sonnets* were "written as a monument."

A failure of memory, but one that brings me to a discrepancy between Hoffmannsthal's "Colours" and my own short narratives, all of which include a she, who plucked the net and sent me traveling. And called me home.

(2009)

Note: The translations included in this essay are the ones I knew first: Hoffmannsthal by Mary Hottinger, Tania & James Stern; Trakl by Michael Hamburger; Rilke by M.D. Herter Norton.

TRIPS NOT TAKEN

::

1.

Which way does your beard point tonight?
—Allen Ginsberg

It's true. Sometimes you don't go. You mean to, but you don't. You say *some other year* and let your plans lapse. Perhaps you already know the trip is dead, that there will be no other year. Perhaps you don't.

And yet, even not going, you realize you have been traveling. Your journey has turned inward. Your eyes have tracked a cloud shadow over a desert basin, the gray-green of a lone tree, a flock of parti-colored goats pushed forward by a boy with a stick, going dark, and then coming alive again, in the sun, when the shadow sails forward. A bit of the shining world subject to tiny eclipse, to resurrection. Or, awake in the night, you listened. In the distance, a siren rose and fell, a pulse, a life ending or a life saved; you couldn't tell, but you were listening to the precarious world, wondering. The everyday world of work and weekends in abeyance. Just you, alone in bed, listening, the mystery of being pressing close.

It's better to travel than not, I think, to endure the way the imagined trip succumbs to the way things actually happen. The foreseen giving way to the seen. The trade you make, must make, traveling, of expectations for surprises, because about the world we are mostly wrong. Imagining it up out of ignorance. Led astray, we do stray. And lost, we find, if not the expected thing, something: Hale-Bopp in a dirty dress, as real as anything from our rooftop in Lahore, but nothing like the balletic beauty pictured in the newspapers. Who were we then, three standing together in a world undeniably tilting toward disaster? We stood and looked together, at the shape of speed, a lovely leap, at our sullied girl stilled in a brown sky. Didn't I feel it, then, a quiet, slow surprise? A bit of the mystery, like a veil, set aside?

I was a partisan of the real. I preferred even the ammoniac reek of a wall yellow with piss to the perfumed dreams sold by travel agents. I preferred the experience to the sell. I still do. Advertisers, what are they but paid liars? And good liars are the worst; they poison our very dreams, as every traveler knows. So I turned against anticipation. I began to travel without preparation, as free of dreams as could be.

About the pleasures of expectation, I grew increasingly baffled. What were they talking about, my friends, when they said half the pleasure of travel was in the anticipation? It seemed mad to prefer the imagined trip to the real trip, but of course that opposition was more than a little neat. Which is what trips not taken finally taught me: the imagined trip is a thing distinct from actually going, an experience of its own and worth having.

::

I'm trying to find the value in a thing most often considered dead loss. It seems obvious that if the imagined trip is the one sold by travel agents, it won't say much about *us*. If we dream the advertisers' dreams, we won't dream our own. It's that simple, in the abstract. But it's worrisome that even travel undertaken solely in our heads should be so endangered by business, by the moneymen who mean to sell us something by first seducing our dreams. Here, too, we must be ready to say *no*, to attend to what we really imagine rather than to what the advertisers are selling.

I'm not suggesting that a traveler imagines up an entire trip before going. The traveler plans, and planning out a trip perhaps only senses at the margins of consciousness the imagined thing. An attraction in flickering images. Intuitions doing their little dance of making sense. Flecks of things. Snow in the mountains, the illusion that a stone house wants to lift off and float into a whitened sky. A close café, windows running with condensation, because there are people there, breathing, huddled up in heavy coats, hands wrapped around hot mugs. Images calling to images, ideas getting born in squalor, the messy beginnings of things. Perhaps the soul's dramaturge gets to work and things happen, there in the mind's eye, among the soft hills and dark canyons. The place is not quite fictional, those are the real landforms of the imagination. And, walking around the near corner of your mind, you can never tell what you are going to find.

::

Mali. We planned to travel in winter, my friend John and I. The dry season, and yet the season least plagued by dust. Dust to clog your lungs and turn your food to mud. Such dust could be daunting, I'd read, blowing out of the Sahara for months, carried by the dry Harmattan. How I love named winds! But having a sonorous name doesn't make a wind pleasant, I knew. I'd suffered the headache Santa Anas in California, hot and smelling of the desert or smoke, and huddled by my small fire in the Balkans, the dread Vardar reminding me that Greece is a colder country than I'd imagined. And winter in Mali has a named wind, too, after all—the Alize—blowing dry and cool out of the northeast, a respite in a parched place. We would go in winter, three weeks or so straddling the new year. That was the plan.

I knew John for a good road companion; we'd traveled together before, in Andalusia. Unflappable, his formidable intellect kept in check by an ecstatic's openness to wonder. He would be traveling first for music, for echoes of Ali Farka Toure, for village *griots*, for the tap and throb of drums, twitching strings, resonant voices singing. Whenever we heard music, I knew John would walk toward it. An enthusiast, he would carry me along into the trance of Malian song. And I liked the thought of that, of music when music turned up, something to interrupt my own abiding obsession with mud, with adobe architecture. John teaches philosophy at the University of New Mexico. For him, adobe is as familiar as a walk across campus or lunch in Albuquerque's Old Town. And it's not far to the pueblos. Not far to the Anasazi ruins at Keet Seel or Mesa Verde. I'd been to the old places, too, and found them impossible to forget. The White House Ruin at Canyon de Chelly hangs still on a sheer face of my imagination. The abandoned villages. The great adobe skeleton that is Chaco, unaccountably left to bleach in the sun these seven hundred years. Somewhere, of course, between the UNM campus and Chaco, an element of strangeness settles in. A familiarity with the kind of construction—with adobe—gives way to the sometimes obscure purposes it was put to, but the biggest difference is that at Chaco the people have gone, the life that included the buildings even as the buildings sheltered it, lost forever.

My desire for Mali assailed me with the first picture I saw of the Friday Mosque at Djenné. It was as if God had knelt down in childhood's sandbox and said, *Watch this...* I knew at once I was called to walk there. You have to walk a building to know how it moves with our passing, and I wanted that, but I was as sure as could be at first glance that the Friday Mosque would support sustained attention. I don't usually like big, and the Friday Mosque at Djenné is the biggest mud building in the world. Reddish earth raised up on the low horizon, the building seems to fan the blue sky, the conical extensions all along the roofline suggesting striations in the air itself. Earth mastering the sky. Earth formed into an image of sentinel attention. I walk a slow circuit around the outer wall. Not too close. There is no reason to get too close. The timbers protruding in rows from the clay plaster enliven the surface of the great walls, register my moving perspective in the way smooth walls would not. On the sunlit sides, they cast bluish, diagonal shadows. Everything happens in relation to the mosque's great presence. That boy pedaling by in a green shirt on his dusty bike, face glistening, he is riding by the mosque, not just riding. Two men in indigo robes, their heads swaddled in white turbans, walking toward each other, they are meeting at the foot of the broad stairs that open the outer wall of the mosque. They are framed by the rounded buttresses that thicken the wall, that make of the steps a passage. They are not just meeting. The city of Djenné stands back from the Friday Mosque, and daily life swirls around it, like the River Bani swirls around Djenné itself. Everybody looks picked out on the open ground around the mosque, their color distinct in the sun against the packed earth. The sheep look very sheepish, what they are somehow more manifest than it would be on cluttered ground. I am walking, the raised waves of the pilasters in the façade rolling forward under my intent gaze, the rows of pilasters set off, more than interrupted, by the three massive rectilinear supports that press out and rise above them. The highest cones, reaching up above the supports and at the squared-off corners of the monumental walls, are each capped by a pearl-white ostrich egg. When I look over at John, he shakes his head, keeping silent. What have words got to do with it, anyway?

On the shady side, the mosque shows starkly against the sun, the warmth of the earthen walls hidden in shadow. But even in winter the air is hot enough that the shade cast by the exterior wall looks attractive, and, indeed, men in twos and threes sit resting there, murmuring or laughing quietly. Because the Friday Mosque is forbidden to infidels, I find that even in my imagination I cannot go in. *Infidel*, nonbeliever, or, worse, faithless. I have sometimes felt a sting in the pity of believers. My kind of confidence doesn't have much currency with them. So we do not climb the steps up, we do not enter. The prohibition is not ancient. Entry was permitted until quite recently, until a French fashion photographer got the bright idea that the smooth lines of the mosque would make a so-dramatic backdrop for photos of his scantily clad models. So beautiful, and the tiny man's little thrill in desecration. Or perhaps just the delusion that his camera gave him the right.

Because I have read that Djenné is not readily accessible by car, the alleys of the city are given over to walkers, to bicycles and push carts. People seeing each other face to face rather than glimpsed behind the glass of their windshields. The wheeling shadows of spokes on clay. Elongated manshapes cast by the sun. Almost everything here showing the trace of the human hand patinated by the weather. This is what I love best. Architecture that has been touched in the making. The solidity and deep recesses of thick, earthen walls. When I run my eye along a roofline or my hand over the top of a wall, I am taken by the sinuous irregularity of the adobe architecture of Djenné, the almost complete absence of machined lines and shiny surfaces. The clay plaster is crackled everywhere except on the most recently renewed buildings. Crackled like the patterns of tree bark, not regularly, but not randomly, either. Where the plaster has failed, the mud bricks underneath show like loaves of bread.

Although the principal beauty rises out of the mud itself—out of the simple forms of the smoothed geometry of the houses, the facades adorned with pillars like legs, with decorative extensions at the roofline like spiky hats or headdresses—all that mud picks out the living. The few trees dignified as emissaries. The loping dog and the strutting goat. And people, each of them standing forth in their condition, humble or exalted. Faces and hands. Feet dusted the color of earth, too. Bright clothes, butterfly blue and dandelion yellow. And when we turn a corner, a small boy greets us from an open door, his knowing eyes sad but friendly. We are lost, but we know we are walking toward water. In Djenné, you are never far from the looping River Bani, from the threaded Niger. We break onto the riverbank, to pirogues nudging the channels. Water in a dry place, it calls to the living. To men and to birds. We are called to the river.

::

In my dream, we ride *bâchées* from Djenné to Mopti and from Mopti on to Bandiagara on the Dogon plateau. A minibus for the first leg, then a big Peugeot. It is the high season, and we don't have to wait long for the *bâchées* to fill. Public transport and stuffed, but such trips imagined are a lot like such trips remembered: time falls out of them. You float over discomfort and the length of the trip. You remember a curious glance or the face of an old man with only one good eye, the way he screwed his head around peering about. The stitched flight of a yellow bird. And, in reality, the run out from Mopti to Bandiagara is not far, a couple of hours on a tarred road.

In Bandiagara, it's no more than two hundred yards from the *bâchée* stop to the Hotel Le Village, where we check in, then shower in a dribble of warm water, our last chance for a bath not out of a bucket until we leave Dogon country. In my mind, we glide through the difficulties. In Sangha, we hire a man who speaks a little English at the *Bureau des Guides*. He wants us to read two well-thumbed letters of recommendation, one written by an Englishman, one by an Australian woman perhaps a bit too enthusiastic. We hire him anyway. Then we are walking, a track along the *falaise*, the great escarpment of the Dogon, the ragged cliffs between the Dogon plateau and the tree-studded Gondo Plain that stretches out to Burkina Faso. In the relative safety of the last few decades, the Dogon have been moving off of the cliffs out onto the plateau, or onto the plain, closer to their gardens. They are small farmers who live by the hoe. The cliffs, which gave them an advantage through centuries of raids, now seem a hard place to get around, impractical. Still, many Dogon continue to live there, and it's the villages on the cliffs we've come so far to see.

We access the *falaise* at Banani but don't tarry, walking away from the main tourist track, which runs south along the escarpment. We steer north to Youga Na. John is a great walker, and I let him go, falling behind a bit. The orange of sandstone cliffs stark against the blue sky. The trail winds along, just a trail and easy, a track in the pumpkin-colored earth, but the world itself is strange here, every tree and lizard unfamiliar, and in that sense more visible. Far overhead, I see the gleam of a jet and, after a gap, a contrail blooming. As if the sky is being plowed by a single share.

All my life I've been criticized for wool gathering, for dreaming, so I'm not surprised when I only notice the two women coming up the trail behind me when they are quite close, when I hear their voices. I step aside to let them pass, women carrying each a great, empty calabash. Perhaps they have sold something in Banani. They hardly give me a glance and then they are by, bare feet orange in the dust, their beautiful indigo skirts and bright, store-bought tops, pink and green, heads wrapped in a twist of cloth. They walk with an easy, upright carriage, and I watch them go. One swings her calabash up onto her head, her raised arm elbow out.

In Youga Na, we sit in the shadow of a baobab tree. Here, there are many. Of all trees, they seem the most human. They do not suggest the young, but old people, gnarled by living. They are mostly trunks, a few twisty limbs and leaves in clumps. They do not cast a thick shade. In a few minutes, we will thread our way through the scree up to the old huts and granaries under the lip of the escarpment. Our guide explains that the granaries were originally built by the Tellem people, who were displaced by the Dogon perhaps six hundred years ago. From where we're sitting, I can see, high up, the cliffs under the overhang riddled with caves and the beautiful geometry of the granaries, which even now are used to store millet and rice. From here, the granaries look like they might have been built by ants or wasps. Many are tall and thin, conical, while others hunker down, squat and boxy.

More than anything, these little structures remind me of Mesa Verde in Colorado, of the granaries built by cliff dwellers in the American Southwest and abandoned by the Anasazi at just about the same time that the Dogon displaced the Tellem along the Bandiagra Escarpment half a world away. In the Southwest, the cliff dwellings persisted, but as ruins. Here, life on the cliffs has remained viable, and I am obscurely moved to see these places inhabited. Here, only John and I gawk. The villagers of Youga Na live here; they are inside this place like an arm in a sleeve, and although we stand among them, we are not. We begin the climb to the cliffs. A couple of small boys with wild smiles race up and down the trail in front of us, amused no doubt by our exclamations, by our bizarre fascination with the commonest things, a bit of carving on a door, the design in plaited mats, by the way mud bricks have been aligned to make a tight seam with the sandstone of the *falaise* where the wall of a hut meets the face of the cliff. The textured surface of the sandstone is not so different than the textured surface of the mud plaster. As we ascend, the paths from the village out onto the Gondo Plain come into view, redder, patterned like a river delta.

It's clear as we climb that here, too, the cliffs are seeing less use, that something like the mysterious migration of the Anasazi away from their cliffs is happening here, right now. Perhaps it is only time that has made the Anasazi's removal mysterious. The reasons for staying became less compelling than the reasons for going. Still, to walk away from such beauty! But the boys don't let me forget that ogling beauty is funny. Looks funny, anyway. But I can hardly believe the ladders set here and there among the cliffs. Arched, sculptural forms, first hacked from tree trunks, the steps have been smoothed and polished by generations of hands and feet. Now they look more like stone than wood, steps running up the back of narrow stone arches. So beautiful. But a little clumsy in boots.

As I understand it, traditional Dogon villages along the escarpment are organized not only by clan but by age; as you grow older, you move up. The oldest male in the village, the *hogon*, lives highest in the cliffs, above him only the burial caves, the abode of the dead. In Mali, the life expectancy is forty-six. So I'm thinking if John and I lived along the *falaise* we'd be enjoying an excellent view over the Gondo Plain, something like this, what we can see now as we climb.

Then we are there, under the overhang, actually standing among the Tellem granaries. And although I know there will be days more walking along the escarpment, that we will be welcomed and eyed warily, startled by the speed of the masked dancing, that we will get a little tipsy on millet beer, that I'll be surprised into new enthusiasms, that I'll feel the music messing with the rhythms of my heartbeat, all that and more, I know that this moment among the granaries is what I've come for. I stop, sit down. John and our guide want to explore, but I'm staying put, sitting with my back against live stone. I went to the Southwest to see the Anasazi ruins, but, beautiful as I found them, they were ruins, and they spoke to absence more than anything else. Absence itself is a way of knowing, of course, and I'd wanted that, but realized as well that the cliff dwellings of the Anasazi would have been very different when the Anasazi themselves were there, rather than a crowd of tourists in dark glasses, shorts, and sunhats.

From where I sit in the cliffs, I can see the Dogon of Youga Na, the real animation of the place, not the ghosts of a people gone, but the living. This is their place, but my seeing is double. Yes, I'm seeing them, the old men in homespun tunics dyed tobacco brown, the traditional cloth caps folded on their heads suggesting the floppy ears of goats. Men like and unlike me. And the young. But I'm also seeing an imaginary landscape, populated too, real too, and not as private as you might think. We dream together, often. We flock together over the same imaginary lakes. We lie down alone or with the same shared lover. It's easy to make too much of the differences. With our various hands we reach into the same bowl. We look up, and time streams across our faces. It's all more common and more mysterious than we care to admit.

A breeze, cooled by the shadows of the overhang, plays over my forehead, my arms. A coolness that feels like light. As if, in the shade, I've begun to phosphoresce. I've grown weary, in the lovely old word *wayworn*, tired of travel. When I first came upon the word, years ago, I imagined it meant the end of travel, that at some point you'd have had enough, and that may yet prove true. But now it seems like an element of travel itself, a part of every journey. Even an imagined journey. And I know for certain that feeling wayworn had a lot to do with why I didn't make the trip to Mali. All through that spring I'd been making plans, investigating what it would take to make a trip to Mali work. Then, in May, I'd traveled to Cambodia. And I'd come back wayworn, my heart worn out, wrung. I didn't expect Mali to challenge my sympathies like Cambodia, but I just didn't feel I could stand another dire-poor place. And when I read that Mali was one of the very poorest countries in the world, my heart balked, and I stayed home.

And yet I kept on reading about Mali, until that too began to feel like a problem. I began to feel I had over prepared, that the trip would be so zoned by expectations I'd never get free of them. And the trip fell away. Later, I realized that if the imagined trip had become an impediment to going, it was itself a compensation, as present as any memory of travel.

If I stay long enough on the cliffs above Youga Na, John and the guide will never come back. In the village down in the scree, where it has pressed from the cliffs onto the plain, twists of smoke will rise up from the cook fires. Later, the mud compounds and the granaries, some wearing their black thatch like a witch's hat, will sink into the darkness, and the cook fires will emerge orange from behind ashes and smoke.

::

I never went to Taxco. I never rode in the white taxies, old VW Beetles with a big red dot painted on the side. The streets narrow and steep. Taxco of the hills. The taxis account for most of the traffic, and they must have been painted to complement the buildings, which have almost all been whitewashed, some of them recently. Many of the exterior walls are painted red up two feet from the ground, banded, a kind of splashguard. And what with the tile roofs that dominate the town, the place is decidedly red and white. And silver. In the old photographs— the black-and-white ones—the palette is, of course, even more restricted. Everything harmonious, the camera insisted. Taken with a large-format camera, printed in silver gelatin, Taxco shows well, gorgeous black shadows and whites so pure they disappear on the paper. In such photos, the world feels distinctly there, present. In spite of the abstraction, the extra abstraction, of black-and-white photography. Perhaps even because of it. If there is less to see in such photographs, what's there feels more available. But you can't travel to this place, even if you go there. And you couldn't have then, when the pictures were taken, either. The situation was not remedied in any fundamental way by the advent of color photography. Indeed, perhaps the pernicious illusion that you can enter the world of the photograph is enhanced even as the felt presence of the image is diminished by color. This is all obvious, and yet it's often photographs we are traveling toward when we set out. We travel toward a world stilled by a camera, motionless and silent. And arriving, sometimes it's the very liveliness of a place that jars us, disturbs the felt presence that we longed for looking at the stills. Those white taxis rattle through Taxco's narrow streets, their engines badly muffled, the air thick with pollution. Tourist music played by sad bands in restaurants, by men in sombreros, makes you want to cry. Some of the picturesque guys sitting on curbs mutter, threatening. Melon rinds rot in untended corners.

And yet, if the silver light in the old prints of Taxco is illusion, the illusion is truer applied to Taxco than it would be elsewhere. Taxco *is* Mexico's silver city, built by silver if not of it: first the silver mines and then the silver jewelry. A thousand shops sell silver in Taxco today. Every day silver is polished and sold winking in the sun in Plaza Borda, the town's main square. Sold by boys out of their pockets under the Indian laurels. Sold off tables and from portable booths. Silver reflections school like fish on the walls of alleys. At my desk, I remember how in Istanbul, in the gold souks of the Grand Bazaar, the bright reflections from the shops gilded the very air, and I imagine something like that must happen in Taxco, too, but silver.

My route to Taxco has been roundabout, nothing so simple as the drive out from Mexico City or up from Acapulco. Those roads now are good, they say. My route passed through a lot of books. I had an interest in the Arts and Crafts Movement, first in American things, which for me meant Mission Oak furniture, then in the related (and mostly earlier) manifestations of the aesthetic in England and Scotland, in Vienna, even in Japan. If I started with furniture, I was soon reading up on the architecture, the decorative arts, about glass and pottery and metal work, and finally about jewelry. My wife gave me a handsome ring handmade a long time ago by the Kalo Shops in Chicago, silver with a jet stone, which led me to Chicago silver, to Harry Dixon out in San Francisco, and somewhere in there I started noticing Spratling silver, beautiful, archaic designs wrought in Taxco. William Spratling, who died in 1967 in a car crash between Taxco and Mexico City, when the roads weren't as good as they are now.

This is all just to say that the road anywhere is likely serendipitous, for me, but for you, too. I read some more, books by Spratling and about him, finishing up with a biography, *The Color of Silver*, which, according to Taylor Littleton, Spratling insisted was white. Spratling came to Taxco traveling and stayed. That can happen. He founded a business in a country not his own and made a lot of money. That happens, too, and looked at closely, often it isn't pretty. The silver mines that built colonial Taxco, after all, were set going by the conquistador Hernando Cortéz, the killer, who found the Aztecs mining there and claimed it all for Spain. You can bet there was plenty of blood in the dross when Cortéz smelted Taxco silver, from which the Spanish minted the coin of empire. Silver from Taxco was struck into coins in the New World and the Old, indeed into coins as far away as Asia. When the mines played out, the costly beauty of colonial Taxco began to crumble. Not a rust belt, but the star in Mexico's silver belt was fast tarnishing to black.

Spratling first traveled through Taxco in 1926; in 1929 he moved there. From the beginning, his vision of Mexico was double. He saw the Spanish Mexico of the conquest and everywhere the surviving signs of the indigenous cultures that Spain had only partially displaced. When, in a move unexpected by all who knew him, he recreated himself in Taxco as a jewelry designer, as a silversmith, he founded his business on pre-Columbian designs. He fostered local artisans. There could be no undoing the damage visited on Mexico by the party of Hernando Cortéz, but Spratling helped to recollect and revalue the design sense of Mexico's indigenous peoples. Spratling's own shops—the *Taller de las Delicias* and later *Spratling y Artesanos*—saw dramatic shifts in fortune in his lifetime. But what he founded was bigger than his own interests. Many of the Mexican silversmiths in his employ became accomplished jewelry designers, too, first copying his designs but subsequently working out their own things from within a design vocabulary clearly derived from pre-Columbian sources. Taxco prospered. And the fabrication of silver jewelry spread from there all over Mexico. In Taxco, Spratling has not been forgotten. There is a silver museum in the city in what was once his home. His workshop at Rancho Spratling in Taxco Viejo now houses the *Sucesores de William Spratling*. So much success has transformed Taxco into one total tourist town, sold by the advertisers as a place to go shopping, shopping for silver. So I hesitated to make the trip, sure as can be that the Taxco of the silver gelatin prints, always an illusion, would now prove doubly illusive. And I wanted to keep the black-and-white city—the stilled Taxco—the Taxco of radical presence—so I didn't go.

And yet I have followed the footsteps of William Spratling as far as a hilltop on the outskirts of Taxco, where I stop. In my imagination, I arrive at noon, the sun is high, the light bright and self-evident. I find a comfortable rock in the dense shade of a small white pine. Taxco is there, its buildings bleaching the very sky above it. Distance, too, quiets a city, and I am keeping my distance. From here I can see the bell towers of the big pink cathedral on the plaza, Santa Prisca, where the priests once stood and raised their wings over Spratling's body, and from where the mourners in their thousands walked with his casket a mile to the grave.

When I stand up, I will turn back, toward the rugged hills to the north. If you look closely, you will see a ring on my right hand. A small slab of lapis lazuli with a cloud floating across it, three big beads of silver on either side, the whole a little irregular, handmade at Spratling's *Taller de las Delicias* before I was born. You won't see me wheel up into the sky like an old man in Chagall, a fat bag slung over my shoulder. That magic is not mine. But even trying to get down to it, to convey the feel of the most common experience—pine needles scratching at the collar of my shirt—for that too some sleight of hand will be required.

::

Every journey suggests another. Road leads on to road. But traveling is one of the ways we learn to value staying home. It makes of home a different place, a place not the best or the worst but one place among many. Your country. Your state. Your town. You begin to taste its distinctive flavor. To keep on going becomes a less attractive thing. You can travel too much. You can lose your home sense, and, like a kite untethered, fall wobbling to the ground.

I think often of a Frenchman I met in a rocky corner of Morocco, deep in the Anti-Atlas Mountains. It was winter and cold. My room wasn't heated, and even the blankets from three beds weren't enough to keep me warm. I wasn't happy or unhappy, but outside of all that, very awake on mornings crusted with glittering frost. Everything a shout. One night, sitting over a bowl of soup in a dirty little cafe, I fell into conversation with the Frenchman, a smallish guy also hunched over a bowl of soup, his hands wrapped around the warmth of the bowl. He was a ragged man in an ochre coat, none too clean. He had a patched quality, and when he talked I noticed his rotten teeth. He told me he'd been traveling for twenty years. He hoped never to stop. He'd grown up somewhere in the south of France—I no longer remember exactly where, Marseilles, perhaps. He seemed to me to have gone feral on the road, but probably he'd always been a little wild. I talked with him only as long as it takes to eat a bowl of soup, to empty a pot of sweet tea. I remember he had reddish hair, bloodshot eyes, a green watch cap. He was moving on in the morning, hitching. I imagined his bones soon bleaching in a ditch somewhere. He was no longer *from* anywhere. He'd lost the tension between home and away. I thought you had to keep that if you wanted to remain a traveler, that without a home place you would be, in some final way, lost. Always the outsider.

But I shouldn't speak so critically about the Frenchman. He didn't want to leave his trips untaken. I can understand that. The far places gleam, beckoning, even if you know for a certainty that half their beauty is mirage. I have not grown so wayworn that the world doesn't shimmer at its edges.

::

2.

> when Charon quit poling his ferry
> and you got out on a-smoking bank
> and stood watching the boat disappear
> on the black waters of Lethe
> —Allen Ginsberg

Life as a journey. It's a commonplace metaphor for our time here on earth, and attractive to travelers. It suggests we've been traveling all along, that any trip in this life is a journey within a journey. The word *journey* itself suggests the trip is short, a day on the road. Just a day and yet a life, which somehow proves to be enough, because the big circles are contained in the little ones. You don't need to travel far to be a traveler.

It was Nikos Kazantzakis who first sent me out seeking in the world. I remember reading that when he traveled he always carried a pocket Dante for a companion book. Such was my admiration for the man that I bought myself a little leather Dante to carry in my own daypack, although, finally, I left it home. I did carry Kazantzakis' picture in my wallet, for years, where another fellow might have kept a photo of his girl. Dante's *Divine Comedy*, I'm thinking now, could be read as a travelogue, an account of a trip not taken. All those dizzying turns down into hell on the initial leg. I like that what Dante imagined was first a journey, and accounts of the life after seem often to involve some traveling. Crossing over. Somebody, maybe, to check your papers at the border, to make sure you're good to go.

About death, too, I have some intuitions, flickering images that visit me in the lulls of living. They are not mine but dreams rising up out of the deeps of culture. Dreams of water. Ebb tide, sometimes. But more often it's a river, the ferryman there, pole in hand. A river heavy as dirty mercury. That river could be the Styx, that ferryman Charon. It's a river. Sometimes I carry a silver coin on my tongue to pay the boatman. Sometimes my body is the boat, a hull of skin wrapped around a box of bones. The mind cool light. The prow rising up like the beak of a bird. The currents dark and sure as gravity. Having arrived, I am ready.

At my desk I think about Allen Ginsberg's poem, "A Supermarket in California," how at the end he questions the dead Walt Whitman, getting no answers. Ginsberg imagines Whitman just stepping off Charon's boat, left alone on the far bank of Lethe, the river of forgetfulness. It's odd that Ginsberg should have imagined Charon plying the waters of Lethe rather than his home river, the Styx. Lethe, it seems you can cross that river before you die. All the lovely mud buildings melting away in the flood. The journeys, the long days, prove surprisingly perishable, glorious and sad.

(2013)

A Note on the Author

Kevin Oderman lives in Morgantown, West Virginia,
with his wife, Sara Pritchard.

BOOKS FROM ETRUSCAN

Zarathustra Must Die | Dorian Alexander

The Disappearance of Seth | Kazim Ali

Drift Ice | Jennifer Atkinson

Crow Man | Tom Bailey

Coronology | Claire Bateman

What We Ask of Flesh | Remica L. Bingham

The Greatest Jewish-American Lover in Hungarian History | Michael Blumenthal

No Hurry | Michael Blumenthal

Choir of the Wells | Bruce Bond

Cinder | Bruce Bond

The Other Sky | Bruce Bond

Peal | Bruce Bond

Poems and Their Making: A Conversation | Edited by Philip Brady

Toucans in the Arctic | Scott Coffel

Body of a Dancer | Renée E. D'Aoust

Scything Grace | Sean Thomas Dougherty

Surrendering Oz | Bonnie Friedman

Nahoonkara | Peter Grandbois

The Confessions of Doc Williams & Other Poems | William Heyen

The Football Corporations | William Heyen

A Poetics of Hiroshima | William Heyen

Shoah Train | William Heyen

September 11, 2001: American Writers Respond | Edited by William Heyen

As Easy As Lying | H. L. Hix

As Much As, If Not More Than | H. L. Hix

Chromatic | H. L. Hix

First Fire, Then Birds | H. L. Hix

God Bless | H. L. Hix

Etruscan Press Is Proud of Support Received From

Wilkes University

Youngstown State University

The Ohio Arts Council

The Stephen & Jeryl Oristaglio Foundation

The Nathalie & James Andrews Foundation

The National Endowment for the Arts

The Ruth H. Beecher Foundation

The Bates-Manzano Fund

The New Mexico Community Foundation

Drs. Barbara Brothers & Gratia Murphy Endowment

The Rayen Foundation

The Pella Corporation

Founded in 2001 with a generous grant from the Oristaglio Foundation, Etruscan Press is a nonprofit cooperative of poets and writers working to produce and promote books that nurture the dialogue among genres, achieve a distinctive voice, and reshape the literary and cultural histories of which we are a part.

etruscan press
www.etruscanpress.org

Etruscan Press books may be ordered from

Consortium Book Sales and Distribution

800.283.3572

www.cbsd.com

Small Press Distribution

800.869.7553

www.spdbooks.org

Etruscan Press is a 501(c)(3) nonprofit organization.

Contributions to Etruscan Press are tax deductible

as allowed under applicable law.

For more information, a prospectus,

or to order one of our titles,

contact us at books@etruscanpress.org.